DRAMAT[illegible]CK!

An Essentially Practical Manual for using Drama in Youth Work

by

DONALD C. STEWART

Russell House Publishing

Dedicated to:

My father who taught me to reach for the stars
To John who showed me the ladder
To Sally who holds it still

First published in 1999 by

Russell House Publishing Limited
4 St George's House
Uplyme Road Business Park
Lyme Regis
Dorset
DT7 3LS

British Library Cataloguing-in-Publication data:
A catalogue record for this book is available from the British Library.

ISBN: 1-898924-22-8

Typeset by TW Typesetting, Plymouth, Devon
Printed by Cromwell Press, Trowbridge

CONTENTS

DONALD C STEWART

Recently appointed Advisor to the Scottish Arts Council Drama Department, Donald C. Stewart has produced over 30 plays and run over 5,000 workshops for young people. With work filmed for presentation on BBC, ITV and Channel 4, this former Director of Community Education at Borderline Theatre Company is now Youth Theatre Organiser for the award winning South Ayrshire Youth Theatre and a Workshop Leader for Scottish Youth Theatre.

ACKNOWLEDGEMENTS

This is a book of love and leisure. In writing the chapters and exercises many stories and reminders have popped into my head to remind me of the exceptional fun and outstanding creativity that was produced through them. I am indebted to thousands. The scripts came courtesy of the following people: Jenny Hainey, Arlene McCreadie, Dave Martin, Jessica McCabe, Suzy McClelland, Val Wilson, Maggot Reid, Nykohla Strong, Chris MacMillan, Richard Caddis, Barry MacLean, Graham Hyslop, Chris Taylor, Colin Johnston, Mark Dempsey, Lynn Barclay, Laura Ann Ward, Amelia Geddes, Ian Henderson, Stewart Graham, Suzanne Holland, Lynne Porterfield, Jonathon Ross, Kirsty Thompson and many, many others who have contributed their time and creative energies into the work which is here ascribed to myself. They come in no order of importance as their personal contribution to my work is measured by their own advancement. To my 'readers' Wilma Beveridge, Patricia McGowan, Ali Kerr, Della Greenwood and my greatest critic and supporter, Sally, thank you.

THE PROLOGUE
AN INTRODUCTION TO THE USE OF DRAMA IN YOUTH WORK

Welcome to **Dramattack!** What follows is a guide to introducing some drama into your youth work. Some might see it as being a pretty brave move but believe me if you can overcome the prejudice then it will bring its own rewards. So don't file it. Read it! Honestly, it'll help. I've found that when you teach people drama, you have to help them to overcome **their** many fears and prejudices of drama. Ultimately everyone seems to have an innate sense of drama being worthwhile but it's what people believe drama is going to be about that stops many of them using it.

So let's start with what I believe drama is. It is *the* most dynamic and passionate means of teaching any subject to young people. I do mean *any* subject. I hope that through reading and using this book you are able to realise that vision too. But remember—what is written here isn't the definitive answer. There are other guides and other methodologies. What I've written is my own guide which I've used successfully for many years. If I succeed in one thing then let it be that you have more questions at the end of this than you had at the beginning.

It is important for you to remember that drama can be used by the complete amateur to spectacular effect as easily as a professional can plan a dramatic event.

Drama gives to people who are described as 'talented', help, training, self-confidence and self-belief that allows them to perform.

In each person there is a valuable human being. If we can truly believe that then the 'untalented', the dispossessed, the '*culturally disenfranchised*' just need encouragement to express themselves. That is what this book seeks to be about and at whom it is aimed. It wants to suggest a framework, some practices, a development which can be used to great effect with young people. I've used the format and others have also. What we have all found is that it can enrich, enliven and entertain. Most importantly it is an introduction to a process.

My failures taught me so much not only about myself but also the 'process' of drama.

For example I once stood in the middle of a school hall surrounded by 20 + members of a local community who had come to 'do drama Mister'. I asked them to gather and start on a warm-up. It was a very large deprived area and the majority of the male members of the group were over 16-years of age and my size or bigger. They sauntered over when I asked and stood in a circle directly in front of me. They peered at me waiting; waiting to be entertained by some 'do-gooder' getting them to dance in tutus! They watched me intently for what felt like an age but was really only seconds. I wasn't prepared for this number or this hostility and my nice wee non-threatening workshop was a disaster.

This experience especially taught me to examine ways in which drama can be channelled correctly.

Why Introduce Drama?

The successes I have had since, showed me drama which, when wed with youth work **can** lead to the full empowerment of groups though self-expression, self-confidence and self-belief. Fine and fancy words as you stand in a freezing hall with the grey paint peeling off the wall bars. You gaze out at their faces peering at you as if you're about to ask them to put on pink tutus and dance *Swan Lake*. It is then that it seems like a million miles away from seeing them enliven debates over serious issues through using a 45-second sketch that's more compact, intelligent and memorable than the Director of Education's 15-minute diatribe. I hope that once you've finished this book you may have your own structure which shall lead to your own successes.

However, when someone else suggests introducing drama then the prejudices of many, many years flow out and the reasons for not introducing it into the group usually end with the line beginning . . . 'if only I could. I mean I realise just how good it is. I remember seeing . . .' I know I've heard it so often.

One of the reasons used against introducing drama (and there are several) comes from our own preconception of what 'drama' actually is? My own experiences are far from unique. To the majority of people drama is a play, curtains, a stage, lights, acting and an audience. Either that or a formalised structure where you're put in your place 'to be educated from the highfalutin culture on-stage'. Let us remind ourselves of what in Britain our very first experience of theatre tends to be. For the vast majority it still comes when we are about four-years old. We feel the excitement of the trip starting when our parents hand us the money for the ticket and we duly trot to nursery school. We pack into buses with our pals and are then taken off to a big place we've maybe seen before when going shopping with our parents. We've certainly never been inside. Up big people's steps to sit in a massive room filled with hundreds of strange people. We hear loud music and clutch our partner's hands so tightly that their circulation halts.

And what's the first thing they do to us? They switch the lights off. Scream? Is it any wonder? We are then treated to a woman dressed up as a man chasing a woman to entertain us. In the meantime 'her' mother is played by a man we might have seen on telly who cracks barely repeatable jokes that at four we don't understand. And people wonder why there are people frightened of using drama!

You see despite our earliest recollections drama doesn't always mean a play, curtains, a stage, lights, acting, an audience or one big pantomime! Drama has many forms. Its processes are varied and complex, however one of the most compelling reasons for using drama may be that unconsciously 'you're using drama already'.

One place you'll find drama is in all of the games played in youth club/activity settings. Not only are almost all of our traditional children's games based on stories (ring-a-ring-a-roses, the farmer wants a wife etc.) but they also have a performance element in their telling. More modern games from songs in the round to complex games (Giants, Pixies and Wizards etc.) contain a 'play' element of let's pretend. Games also have rules and rituals of performance, which have similarities in drama. Find games you play and you've also found drama, which is why '*you may be using drama already*'.

How to Start Using Drama

As a tool to engender discussion amongst groups—particularly young people—drama is great. You may find that you have lots of special moments, which, if strung together, may form the basis of a particularly good play. You may also find that the many timorous people who came along are now to be augmented by people principally attracted not for social welfare reasons but for dramatic/artistic ones.

I look back at my own participation and see myself standing neither in a school hall nor in a community centre. I see myself on a stage.

I got involved because I wanted to act. I wanted to perform. I wanted people to applaud me because I was good. The fact is that there is absolutely nothing wrong or egotistical in wanting to perform. I can see exactly why young people can become transfixed by the lights—I was.

As an actor there is nothing wrong in the desire to perform, but as a youth leader or teacher in charge of a group who wish to perform it is a large undertaking to work towards a production. We shall look at these issues later, whether you want to perform or not, at the end of your project. It is important to consider before you start why you want to use drama and also to what end. You may wish to consider whether or not you want 'a performance'. You have to start by being realistic and also what expectations you are likely to raise. I mentioned before that you may already be using drama and later on I suggest one way of introducing 'dramatic concepts' into your youth work. You can build up a bank of ideas which can then be 'turned into' a dramatic piece of work even though they don't at first seem to have anything to do with drama at all. Strangely enough this is mirrored in professional theatre—the first rehearsal should never end up looking like what appears on-stage. This book is designed to help you through two choices.

We define these two choices as between **Workshops** and **Performances**. I would suggest that the easiest way to decide which of the two you wish to do is to decide whether you want your group to perform in front of a live audience. There are deeper theoretical/philosophical arguments for each but you want to stick to the simple. **workshops** exists for themselves and are conducted over usually a short given time frame. Such self-contained units can be loosely or tightly structured and lead to self-expression within a group. **Performances** are lengthy in preparation with much organisation, having many people involved in their process. They can lead to sacrifices being made in favour of getting the job done but lead to group bonding and self-confidence through achievement.

How to Use This Manual

We shall start by explaining how you can put into the work that you currently do, some drama, which can then be added to through role play and improvisation towards potentially some form of performance. However, although there would seem to be a natural progression there, doesn't need to be. Having started your group thinking in a dramatic way you may want to introduce a 'drama workshop'. There are several from which to choose. For the more challenging artists there are then *Integrated Workshops* that develop the workshop theme further. The integrated workshop introduces the concepts of a performance within a workshop. It can last nearly two hours without any rehearsals! If you want to perform or are in the middle of rehearsals right now then it's straight to the Act 2, which deals specifically with performing.

But you will need the help of **Bob**. He'll pop up throughout the book in various guises. They are:

Full figure: When he appears like this it's essential you read the chapter or the introduction before doing any of the exercises.

Head, shoulders and 1 raised finger: This is an exercise that's easy.

Head, shoulders and 2 raised fingers: This is a more complicated exercise and may need an exercise done before you attempt it.

Head, shoulders and 3 raised fingers: This is the drama badge. You're nearly expert and this needs preparation and some feeling of comfort with drama.

You decide where you are and remember we're trying to guide you. You can mix and match and please, please, please ignore me if you think you can get better results by doing so.

Contained therein are just a few perceived wisdoms, which have been culled from years of working with young people and trying to make them look good under spotlights. There are several more ideas which you might not already have thought of which will come in handy as you continue to rehearse. The most important part of this book is that it is supposed to give you ideas and not to solve all of your problems. Please don't think I have covered all of it—I never will that's why it's so damned exciting. Fancy joining the journey? Then read on Macduff.

ACT ONE, SCENE 1
AN INTRODUCTION TO WORKSHOPS
It's Drama Jim but not as We Know it . . .

Introduction

So you want to introduce drama but don't want to do *Hamlet* just yet! But if drama is not about performing then what is it? Drama is **not** always all that it appears to be. It is **not** meant to be threatening and it is certainly **not** only for the **'talented'**.

Whilst drama is conventionally seen as a play, with curtains opening and shutting on a stage, with lights illuminating the action, with actors pretending to be someone else, mainstream drama has professionally swept the cobwebs from the corners of these notions.

For example, drama without a script is an improvisation; without curtains it's done on an open stage; without a stage it is done in promenade; without lights it can be street theatre; without 'acting' it is done naturally; it is never however without an audience (although there are experimentalists who will tell you that it is!). The mistake we make is to assume that the audience is always the one sitting waiting for the play to begin whilst in the auditorium. They don't need to be.

Drama's audience is not therefore always the fee paying public. Very often the audience can be made up of those participating. It is a structured activity following a pattern which does make it different from chaos. Hopefully, in the *Introduction* I demonstrated why people ought not to be frightened of drama. We must however remember that, particularly young people can be suspicious of drama.

Less confident people, particularly, young people are stopped from achieving because they are put off by others. It is the job of enablers to counter this.

People can equate uppity children who can whistle *White Christmas* whilst accompanied by their favourite aunt on the spoons with screen stars at the late night Friday showing; men and woman whose eyes convey emotion without the need to rely on cheap music hall gimmicks. It is particularly important to remember that you have young people there voluntarily.

Apart from being a means in themselves it can be a means through which you can introduce drama, even surreptitiously without a performance or worrying about the 'talented'.

Drama workshops introduce the idea that drama is for all and to be enjoyed by all. Thousands of 'untalented' people turn up for community drama sessions.

If you believe that acting a role is something that you can do everyday and that you are convincing in that role—you can act well. We all manage to act as ourselves utterly convincingly **all day** after all. To act as someone else you may only need to learn the technique of changing one aspect of yourself. Once learned, like all other techniques, constant rehearsal and practice keeps it alive and in trim. For an athlete to consistently perform well they must train; so too must an actor. Once you demystify the process, see how uncomplex it becomes!

Workshops are a vital element in the process of drama. A workshop allows you to focus on various aspects of performance and even to perform miniature playlets for rehearsal purposes. I have attended many 'workshops' run at conferences, seminars and training events which were little more or less than a mini-lecture involving an overhead projector, or a flip chart and sedentary participants. Drama workshops are not the same. Drama workshops seek to engage all participants equally and with participation as the key.

Characteristics of an effective and enjoyable workshop include:

- Practically involving the participants.
- Structured activity.
- Being very noisy.
- Looking chaotic and badly managed.
- Having participants as the focus—always!

These are by no means exhaustive and workshops may contain even more elements than these. Let us take these elements one at a time before we get down to the practical application of them.

Participants are Practically Involved

Workshops must involve your participants in creating something whether for themselves or for others. You want each participant to have achieved something for themselves. It may be that they have managed to muddle through act one, scene two of *Hamlet* or they have responded creatively to a piece of music. It may merely be a few games through which they have learned the discipline of following rules or the creativity of breaking them.

They are Structured

There is a basic structure under which I gather my material. It is not the be all and end all of doing drama and there are many other creative people who would balk at the very thought of being boxed in by a set of structures. However to not consider it so in youth work is to send youth workers into situations without the safety net of plan B which could turn workers and participants off drama forever.

They are Usually Noisy

Don't expect when you ask even two people to form creative groups that they will do so silently. It is also important that when there are people coming to view what you are doing that they don't expect to see hundreds of little groups working silently in an ordered fashion. Creativity makes noise. It also does so selfishly without noticing whether or not they are disturbing others. That's just great!

They Look Chaotic and Badly Managed

But they are not, as we shall see from the structure! I often walked into other teachers' classrooms when I taught. There was something then described to me as a working noise. I believe that this exists. In drama workshops too there is a very real 'working atmosphere' which in looking at it from the outside can look as though no one is in control. If the youth leader looks relaxed you can bet that they are very much in control.

Participants are the Focus—*Always!*

If you find yourself talking too much and your group sitting and watching you for hours, you are doing something very wrong. Remember the performance must be from them and **not** from you. It is specifically an opportunity for them to create and must be seen as such.

The Structure

The structure on which I base each of the workshops can be easily sketched out. It is:

1. **Warm-ups.**
2. **Theatre games.**
3. **Techniques.**
4. **End games.**

Let's start with *Theatre Games* in Scene 2 before looking directly at the overall drama structure. In sport, young people will want to 'play' the game but not warm-up for it unless they are serious participants. So too in drama, warm-ups tend to be the preserve of the 'theatre interested'. Drama can be introduced into youth work without the need to announce 'next week we're doing drama' and then be left wondering why no one turned up. You can gently introduce a 'theatre' game every so often or weekly until a small batch of such games is known by the group. Let's begin there then . . .

ACT ONE, SCENE 2
THEATRE GAMES
If Drama be the Food of Love, Play on . . .

I said earlier that you may be using drama already. The next few games allow you to begin to plan and introduce concepts which will help build up a bank of drama concepts without referring to them as such. It is these concepts which you will make use of later. It is important to note that we are not asking people to 'do drama'. The reason I suggest that you're using drama already is because all games have elements of performance involved in them, including rituals or rules, which are the same/similar to the rules of theatre.

I attempt to build up games with a group which create a structure, and can then be used through that **structure** and allow you to sneak the drama theory in without frightening anyone—particularly yourself!

Later I look at drama workshops without an obvious structure but which have a tight informal structure and will make use of the same concepts and structures of games outlined here. I therefore work towards using games dramatically rather than as 'fillers'.

Games at the Beginning of the Session

Games of tig* involve chases. If you split up the complex versions into different types you can see more easily the dramatic developments which are possible as you progress through them. This will allow you to see how games have theatrical outcomes.

Let's look at the simple basic rules of tig first. It is a game where one person/some people attempt to 'tig'/touch another person thus 'catching' them. Once that action has taken place the chasing person may change with them/knock them out of the game/transfer them onto their own side/await the result of a forfeit. Even a simple game of tig where there is one catcher can be played in different ways in different parts of the country. This is generally why the basic definition can lead to countless possible ways of being played. I have sorted them into seven headings:

1. **Simple Chase Tigs**
2. **Character/Action Tigs**
3. **Word Tigs**
4. **Line Tigs**
5. **Cat and Mouse**
6. **Complex Physical Tigs**
7. **Complex Cerebral Tigs**

Now let's look at each of the games in turn. If you play one game five times, you could convert an entirely random result into a performance. How? Simple. Instead of

**'Tig' is in some areas referred to as 'tag' but in Ayrshire it's 'tig'!*

two teams you may have two rival villages, or two marauding armies. You can then replay the entire random game with the same events as just played out with a narrator explaining the story. Extending it further could be interviewing with ITN on the battlefield with Chief McPixie of clan A or whoever. Eyewitness reports after the carnage; pundits in the studio before tig-off, etc. Here are the games with further examples. They are **far** from exhaustive.

1. Simple Chase Tigs

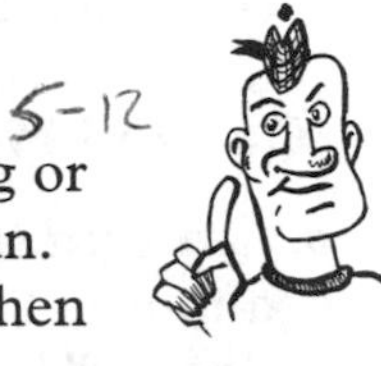

- ***Hospital tig:*** When the catcher tigs someone they hold the part tug or hobble or limp as if hurt. The game ends when all are unable to run.
- ***Cruel tig:*** Same as hospital tig but each place tug falls off. Only when both legs get tug is the person 'out'.
- ***High tig:*** Slightly different physically because you can escape the catcher by escaping somewhere high. (One variation is Pirates where wall bars, mats etc. are brought out and a 'gym jungle' or 'gym ship' is created for people to escape in when chased. Anyone tug or who falls off onto the floor is out as they are then in shark infested waters.)
- ***Low tig:*** As you can imagine the opposite type of escape from *high tig*. You have to crouch low as your escape.

2. Character/Action Tigs

- ***Mummy tig:*** When tug the person caught must walk like an Egyptian mummy. Game ends when everyone is walking like that. Other character tigs include Dracula, Frankenstein, spaceman, superhero or any theme you can think of!
- ***Dead fly tig:*** When tug, lie flat on your back waving your arms and legs in the air. Freed when someone touches their nose on your nose. (Nose to nose contact—watch drippy noses! This is a good game to end a physical session on as everyone ends up sitting down.)
- ***Tunnel tig:*** When tug stand still with legs open. Freed when someone crawls through your legs.
- ***Aeroplane tig:*** When tug stand still with arms outstretched. Freed when someone runs underneath your arms.
- ***Statue tig:*** Children stop still as a statue when tug.

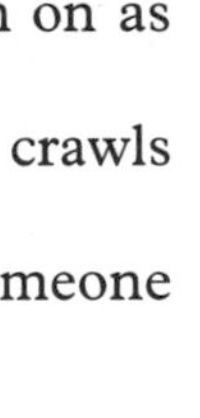

3. Word Tigs

- ***Video tig:*** Children are safe when they sit down and shout out the name of a video.
- ***Bully tig:*** Children are safe when they shout out a rule to avoid being bullied.
- ***Pop star tig:*** Children are safe when they shout out a favourite pop star.

4. Line Tigs

- ***What's the time Mr Wolf?:*** Everyone stands in a line. Mr Wolf stands with their back to the line. Everyone chants 'What's the time Mr Wolf?'. Mr Wolf shouts out the time at each request. The time of day decides

the number of steps forward everyone must take (e.g. **four** o'clock means **four** steps). When Mr Wolf shouts 'dinner time' they turn and chase the others and try to catch someone before they cross back over the line. Then you have a new Mr Wolf.

- ***Poison:*** Someone holds their hands out and everyone takes a finger. That person tells a story. When they say the word 'poison' everyone flees and the one 'tug' becomes the storyteller. If everyone gets to a corner of the room before being 'tug' they then are safe and the storyteller stays who they were.

5. Cat and Mouse

- ***Cat and mouse:*** The 'cat' is chasing all the 'mice'. When they catch a mouse the mouse goes in a 'cage' (an area marked with chalk on the floor). When a free mouse stands in the cage and counts to three, all the other mice in the cage go free.
- ***Tails 1:*** Everyone has a tail tucked into their trousers at the back. When the cat (who has no tail) pulls it out the mouse is 'dead' or eliminated.
- ***Tails 2:*** Everyone again has a tail and one chases and takes tails. Every mouse with tail taken becomes a cat. Game ends when everyone has lost a tail.
- ***Half and half:*** Half of the mice have one colour tail, the others have another. Mice chase mice and at the end of the game the 'team' with the most tails from the other group is the winner.
- ***Grid cat and mouse:*** Everyone apart from two or three people stands in a grid holding the hands of the people to left and right of them. The two or three people excluded become a cat and mouse/mice. The mice are released into the grid with the cat following. Neither are allowed to break the holding hands of people in the grid. When the leader shouts 'change', the grid changes 90° and everyone holds hands with new partners. Game ends when mouse/mice is/are caught.

6. Complex Physical Tigs

- ***Giants, pixies and wizards:*** Split the group into two halves. The game is very similar to paper, scissors and stones but has a physical element. Each half decides whether they are all giants, pixies or wizards. The two groups then form two lines about five paces apart and at a given signal they walk forward towards the middle and recite '**ishkaboodle ishkaboodle one, two, three**' and 'show' what they are—giants, pixies or wizards.
  —**Giants** have two hands straight up in the air or cross their arms.
  —**Pixies** have two arms above their heads in a triangle or waggle their fingers under noses going 'shshshshsh'.
  —**Wizards** 'spray' their hands like spells and shout 'zap!'.
  —**Giants** are scared of **pixies** and are chased by them.
  —**Pixies** are scared of **wizards** and are chased by them.
  —**Wizards** are scared of **giants** and are chased by them.

Whichever half is to be chased must get to the wall, stage, edge of badminton court or wherever at their side before being tigged. If caught they then join the other side.

The game ends when all the children are in one team, this is a good place to stop if you are bored or things are not quite working.

- ***British bulldog:*** One person stands in the middle asking someone to cross from one side of the hall to the other. If that one person gets passed then everyone must cross. Anyone tug on the way over becomes a catcher.
- ***Trees in the woods:*** Two groups opposite each other run as fast or as slow as possible to the opposite sides. Any two who touch become frozen trees. They must then stand rigid and tig anyone who crosses on subsequent turns. Anyone tug becomes a tree.
- ***Red rover:*** One person in the middle of the hall calls 'red rover, red rover—we want (name) over'. That person must get past the catcher and if they don't then they have to choose the next person and so on until everyone is 'out'.

7. Complex Cerebral Tigs

- ***Cerebral tig:*** Everyone imagines in their head who is 'het'. They then must tig everyone including that person and sit down to win. If they get tug by that person they lose. Very interesting if two people choose each other to be 'het'.
- ***Paranoid fish:*** Sculpture game where everyone must work out in their own mind who is 'het' and who is their best friend. In a limited space count 5 to 1. On 1 they must get as close to their best friend as possible and as far away from the 'het' person. Very interesting when best friends turn out to think you're 'het'!

These basic games of tig are drama games. How? There are three important reasons. The first of these reasons is that games teach us rules. Rules which provide structures to follow. Those structures create two possibilities—staying within them or expanding out with them.

If you take any of the tigs there is a mutual understanding that is unbroken, that the game to be achieved must be played in a 'certain' way. The games will always have limits. Drama can seek to challenge and change those rules/limits by extending outwith them. New games can be created by someone suggesting a new rule or by suggesting the abandonment of another. However we start by introducing the concept of a structure. It has its parallels in acting.

Now imagine yourself on a stage. You have got there through the rules—rehearsal, direction, learning your lines etc.—and yet you are not performing quite as you would want. The rules may be constraining you and you find that the performance may not be quite ready. Like the child who suggests the new rule, you suggest saying the first line a different way. The child gains a new game, you a new performance. That creative mindset is why games like tig are important to drama—because they teach us tricks to learn by. Games exercise our creative side. We're figuring out how to get away; whether we can reach the wall; what will happen if we do or don't stay free so we create a mindset and rehearse our creativity.

The second reason why they are drama games is because they are dramatic. Drama comes from conflict. It is defined as 'the resolution of conflict through the adoption of character'. One person against the rest is dramatic. At least half of Hollywood is based on that concept!

The third reason is they can be hidden stories themselves. Let me take one game to demonstrate :

Hospital Tig

The Game

James is 'het'. James is one of the most popular kids in your group. Right from the beginning a number of the girls are deliberately being caught. James is tigging arms and legs meaning that girls are hobbling about. James is then catching boys out but his greatest rival John is still not caught. James has him in his sights and decides that he's going directly after him. Wading through most of the group who are now on the floor clutching arms and legs, James is cornered but gets out because you call an end to the game.

The Drama

James and John enter and look at each other across the room. The rest of the group scatter then decide to stop the showdown. James 'tigs' and downs each of the people he did in the game except this time rather than in a frantic game it happens systematically one by one until their injuries litter the room. Just as James arrives at John for the showdown, James smiles, lifts his hand and switches to 'away' his remote control for his time machine and leaves.

The point of the exercise is to show how the result of a game might allow a dramatic interpretation because the structure of the conflict is dramatic. The basis, theory, philosophy of drama is taught by experiencing the concepts challenging them and creating new structures. By playing games we stimulate our creative thinking, even at the most basic—a child's playground game.

Tig's element of chasing can be also used to introduce difficult concepts. One further example is Shakespeare. The character Juliet, at the age of 13, was written by Shakespeare for a young man to play the part. For a 13-year old in the 21st century to fully understand how to fall in love is very difficult for them. If you want an example of how daft, see Boal's *Games for Actors and Non-Actors*. And yet Romeo is chasing Juliet while Juliet wants to be caught. Now replay the balcony scene as a bad game of high tig! It may not change how you would stage it but it may bring young people more understanding of the adult or more mature themes.

The third reason is that tigs can therefore be built over a period of time towards a drama or introducing drama. It is sneaky, but goes back to what I said earlier. Drama is often not used because of fear of the product or of performance or ignorance of the process involved in just creating. Understanding the process is not frightening and a product—the drama workshop—is born. If you introduce over say five or six weeks some wee games of tig then the introduction of more and more drama based games later becomes easier. A six week programme could look like the one on page 13.

There are further games coming up which may be used and have a dramatic structure. Using them means they become part of your drama 'bank' which each individual member of the group may share. Thus you begin to build an understanding of concepts which eventually will lead to them communicating with their audience whoever they may be, more effectively.

	Week 1	**Week 2**	**Week 3**	**Week 4**	**Week 5**	**Week 6**
Length of activity	10 mins	15 mins	15 mins	15 mins	20 mins	25 mins
Game	*Hospital tig*	*Mummy tig*	*Tree tig*	*Bully tig*	*Poison tig*	*Telepathic tig*
Type	Physical	Physical	Physical	Cerebral	Game	Drama
Game	*Low tig*	*Aeroplane tig*	*Statue tig*	*Giants, pixies and wizards*	*Telepathic tig*	*Paranoid fish*
Type	Physical	Physical	Cerebral	Game	Drama	Drama
Game	*Dead fly tig*	*Video tig*	*Trees in wood*			
Type	Physical	Cerebral	Game			

I have used the primary playground game of tig. Many young adult groups may find the idea of playing tig absurd. There are other games therefore apart from tig, which can be played. However many 14/15-year olds will play a complex physical game. If you analyse them you may find their origins back in the primary school playground!

Games for the End of a Session

Another place to sneak wee drama games in is at the end of the evening session. Indeed any session where there are time fillers used will have games with dramatic overtones. The point of workshops is usually to end on a high note and there are games which I suggest here to do that.

Rules Games

- ***Wink murder:*** There are quite a few versions of this game. My favourite is to line everyone up with their backs towards you. You tig a murderer and a detective. Everyone then wanders around and when the murderer winks at you, you're dead. The detective has three tries to find them.
- ***Guess the rule in the round:*** Everyone sits in a circle and you pick someone to leave. When they've left you decide on a rule that, when you answer a question you will abide by that rule. The person you sent away returns and has three guesses to find out what that rule is.

Games in the Round

- ***Bear and the honeypot:*** One person is a bear with a set of keys beside them. Everyone else is in a circle around them. You touch one of the children in the circle and they must steal the keys, go out the circle through the place where they were sitting, run round and back to their place. The bear must chase them. If they get caught then they become the new bear. The bear starts to chase as soon as they hear the keys move.
- ***Buzz:*** This is another simple in the round game where you count from one to whenever, with the word 'buzz' being substituted for numbers divisible by three, or four, or five etc. You also have to say 'buzz' when the number you are basing the times table on is mentioned. So 3, 13, 23 etc. are buzz words when playing with

three. People are put out when they get it wrong, so you can use it as a building exercise with the group out when they get it wrong and they have to get to a prearranged number like 100 together.

- ***Going shopping:*** When you go shopping you collect something beginning with an **a**. The person next to you collects what you said and then something beginning with a **b**. The person next to them must remember what **a** and **b** were before giving a **c** word. Then the next person builds it and so on throughout the alphabet.
- ***Minister's cat:*** Adverbial version of the game this time with the minister's cat described as an adventurous cat then a boisterous cat and so on. In the *minister's cat* there is no need to remember all of the adverbs as you go round. One at a time will do!
- ***Chinese whispers:*** An old favourite, where you whisper in someone's ear something which they then repeat to the next person and so on until you get to the end of the group and hope that some gibberish comes out. I must confess to never knowing what to say at the beginning.
- ***Chinese mime whispers:*** This is a physical version of *Chinese whispers*. You send up to four people out of the room. You then show the group a mime. They guess what it is and then you bring the first of your four people sent out back. You show them the mime and they must show it to the second, the second to the third, the third to the fourth and the last one must guess what was happening. Use a simple activity with clear movement. Examples include—making an omelette, planting seeds etc.

Some end games are more obviously 'dramatic lead' than tig games and could be slotted into an evening, somewhere around week 3 of our previous plan. Something of this order could work out:

	Week 3	**Week 4**	**Week 5**	**Week 6**
Length of activity	15 mins	15 mins	20 mins	25 mins
Game Type	*Chinese whispers* Round	*Chinese mime whispers* Round	*Chinese mime whispers* Round	*Bear and honeypot* Round
Game Type			*Name game* Round	*Buzz* Round
Game Type				*Minister's cat* Round

By following the plan suggested, by week 6, 45 minutes of your session could have a drama base. Now you have established a beginning and an end. What should you fill in between?

Games for the Middle Bit

Character Games

- ***Who am I?:*** You are allowed to answer *yes* or *no* to questions asked by your group as they attempt to work out who you are. It must be someone famous enough that they will know them and I would suggest a time limit if the session begins to drag.

- ***Hot spot:*** When we ask actors to create a character we use a technique known as hot spotting. All that happens is that we put the actor in the centre of a circle and we ask them all sorts of questions about themselves. A tremendous amount of fun can be had as well as some unusual answers!

Trust Games

N.B. Trust games are highly worthwhile but you must be comfortable with their use. Do not attempt to use them if you feel at all that your group may not take to them or that you are nervous about possible injury. (That includes to yourself!) It is not wise to judge them on the basis that you wouldn't trust the group if you were blindfolded—if we measured all youth work that way we wouldn't do very much now would we?

- ***Blindfold the animals:*** This is an introduction of the concept of listening, which becomes very important with the obstacle courses. We give each member of the group a card with an animal on it. They are then blindfolded or they are asked to close their eyes. They then have to find another person with the same animal on their card by making the animal noise whilst trying to find them. You can have three pigs, four sheep or set numbers. It is up to you whether or not you tell them how many are out there of each type, but sometimes it can be quite interesting to see if they manage to work out if they have collected together all of their same type.
- ***Obstacle course***
  —***Single:*** Set up a course from one end of the room to the other with overturned chairs, tables in the way, chairs to be walked over the top of and so on. Ask the group to split themselves into smaller groups of say six or seven. They number themselves and you ask one at a time to come to the beginning of the course and be guided blindfolded from the beginning to the end. Their team from their group must shout instructions to them.
  —***Groups:*** You follow the same pattern as when they play as singles except this time you are asking all groups to go at the same time.
- ***Lean back:*** The group stand in a circle surrounding one member of the group. The one in the middle then leans back onto the hands of each member of the group who have to gently pass him or her from hands to hands and round in a gentle circle.
- ***Drop in!:*** This is the same almost as *lean back* except you are working in pairs. One person stands with their back to the other and drops backwards onto their hands. Always fascinating to see if there are any partners willing to fall almost to the floor.

One obvious word of caution comes again with the trust games—use them very carefully. If you don't have the trust of your group then you won't find it easy to run trust games. It is certainly not a good idea to do trust games if you are not insured against personal injury claims.

Exclusion Drama Games

- ***Rules games:*** This is another game in the round, where this time a member of the group leaves the room and everyone decides that they will answer any question asked of them by observing a certain rule. The excluded person wins if in three guesses they work out what the rule is. An extension of this, which can take hours and be quite frustrating and fun is playing this as a whole group versus another whole group. Group one are told that they are now called number 1, 2, 3 etc. and they must answer any question as the person opposite them. The other group must then sit opposite and, in turn ask questions of Group one. It can take ten minutes or it took me two hours to work it out!
- ***Crossed and uncrossed:*** This is a passing game and one which can again be quite fun. You are passing scissors from one person to another whilst answering questions on what the rule is. When the scissors are passed whether they are crossed or uncrossed is immaterial as the answer comes from whether the recipient's *legs* are crossed or uncrossed. You are therefore passing the scissors round a circle and you alone are commenting on the crossing or uncrossed part of the equation. When people think they know what the answer is they must whisper it to you. The game finishes when everybody has worked it out.

We are now ready to look at purely dramatic techniques. These are directly dramatic and use role play, hot spot and other theatre techniques.

One of my favourite games is the all over body warm-up tig. Tig is a wonderful game. It is full of variations which, when played, can release pent up energy as well as demonstrate the dynamics of a group.

Although drama can be seen as a cerebral activity—acting, music and even dance or circus—it can still require a physical exertion which is slightly above our normal daily routine. Anyway who says we shouldn't warm-up our brains before we start using them?

ACT ONE, SCENE 3
ROLE PLAY
Roles without Ham!

- **Warm-ups.**
- **Theatre Games.**
- **Theatre Technique.**
- **End Games.**

Having covered games let's turn ourselves to theatre techniques. Theatre techniques are basic tricks of the trade or exercises directly concerned with the cut of drama—role play, character work, circus skills etc. Once you've worked in the concepts and ideas with games what are you going to do now? After all we want to introduce drama. The two easiest ways are *Role Play* and *Improvisation.*

Role play is the structurally more sound and easier to do. This is because of the pre-planning. If you're involved in drugs/alcohol/any subject type of informal youth work you'll know how much preparation goes into an Awareness Evening just to make sure you can answer nearly every question. Role play can, and often does, involve that level of preparation. The other, improvisation, is more free, more open and therefore is often better liked by dramatists. Both involve an element of 'giving away' control however whilst improvisation can be pure free fall, role play is a bit like falling out of the plane with that cord still connected. Role play involves members of your group playing predetermined roles created by you in situations which you have created. Improvisation involves your group in creating their own characters within situations which may or may not be predetermined. We are going to concentrate on role play first.

Role Play—Introduction

This is where the language of theatre does becomes important. When people play a part in a play they adopt a 'character'. They 'play' a role. To play 'in character' is seen by some as the main 'purpose' of theatre. We're talking about what is generally perceived as 'acting'. We start with a definite character say, a Teacher. The character could be strict; a disciplinarian; their clothing crisp and efficient. For further identification we may top them with a mortarboard and cloak to dress them. The situation that could be used is this 'character' disciplining someone who has transgressed a minor school rule or other. Our 'play' would become acting that scenario out with the proposed object of the drama to be either challenging that rule or demonstrating a valid reason if any exists for having the rule. Although it may be obvious through the use of a stereotype that it is the latter we wish to prove. We may wish however to find another stereotype for the teacher character such as the teacher who cannot control the class to demonstrate other rules or modes of behaviour.

It is essential to realise that with role play we give structure within which young people can start to create. They then use these tools to put across a point or attempt to demonstrate a particular absurdity.

I always start with a definite dramatic scenario. Once I have that scenario for role play I need to have a tight structure to follow with character types; roles that characters are placed in; and developed situations related to their characters in which they play out their dilemmas.

We then need to have a look at those dilemmas.

One common reason for using role play is that a problem has arisen which requires some solution or investigation. It is a problem which sometimes is solved by posing the question 'how would you feel if this happened to you?'. Your group, however, may require to understand more than 'this is a bad thing to do' and to realise what the root of the problem and perhaps where the solution is. You may want to explore with them *why* and *how* as well as *what*. The scenario may well be one that is simple at first telling, however it may require more detailed examination. As an example let us take the dilemma of stealing.

The Role Play Dilemma

You have your dilemma: someone is stealing. However, for role play that is not nearly enough information. You need to know more. Remember earlier in the example of the teacher, it may be to prove a rule or to demonstrate how absurd it is. Let us create some fictional facts—the scenario.

The fictional scenario may be that someone is constantly stealing from a local shop on the way to the youth club. They have done so every week for the last four weeks. One member of the youth club knows what is going on and there are rumours that the shopkeeper suspects someone at the youth club but is not sure what their name is. The shopkeeper approaches the youth leader on the fifth week and fifth occurrence. The youth Leader has a dilemma. The shopkeeper wishes to organise an identity parade so that they can pick out the culprit and have them arrested. The youth leader doesn't believe that this will help in any way. They refuse but assure the shopkeeper that they *will* bring any thief to justice. The shopkeeper, for the moment is satisfied by the youth leader's sincerity.

Preparations

You have your dilemma but an incomplete story. My primary five teacher always said start with *who, what, where, why and when*? So . . .

who are involved? the thief, the pal, the shopkeeper and the youth leader. **Characters**

What is the problem? Stealing. **Dilemma**

Where are we concerned with? The shop; the youth club (we can complicate it a wee bit by adding someone's home). **Places**

Why do we want to look at this topic? someone in our club might be stealing. **Scenario**

From when do we wish to look at this issue? When the shopkeeper approaches the youth leader. **Time**.

We need, however, to look at some of them in more detail before we start.

Why do we want to look at this topic? Why is also the point we want to investigate. OK so we can deal with absolutes such as '*stealing is wrong*' on the surface but what if the thief is also a victim? A role play may hinge on that question mainly because someone, who will play the thief may want and deliberately try to scupper your work to extend their character by having some credible defence. 'Why' must therefore take in all sorts of possible avenues and scenarios which will be explored by your group.

Sometimes we plan scenarios and dilemmas to the nth degree only to find our group is far more creative than we are!

When do we wish to look at this issue? Today—it's immediate. The other 'when' question is when in your youth work programme? Once we have established in their minds the structure of 'playing games' with rules and rituals we can start to work in dramatic structures so perhaps in week 5 of 6 as suggested above. You must work on your situations in advance to redraft as many avenues you can and work on them until you are confident that you have as many questions answered in your own mind as is possible prior to using it with your group. This is particularly important if you are new to using drama or role play. A seasoned user will probably be using straight improvisation! The novice would find it hard to handle. You will therefore want to acquaint yourself well with your group in advance!

It is important to start by thinking of all the possible connotations. For role play it is a good discipline to start off by developing your first role play before using it. If you do not you may end up with the policy decision or challenge you can't answer. Wherever you work role play can throw up awkward situations. You can be challenged on what you would do if someone was actually stealing from the youth club or if someone made a serious allegation against another youth club member of just how confidential little chats are. Check before exposing yourself to such possibilities!

The questions posed in our situation with the thief will therefore open up others as it is supposed to. The questions are not ones of circumstances but of real people; of imagined responses; of fictional roles.

The most important part in any role play is always therefore the *who are involved?* After all it is a role play—a character exercise. To attempt to role play without having a clear understanding of who is to be involved can make for difficulties. Do you want groups of four people to involve a teacher or a janitor; a parent or another school friend? Are they going to be sympathetic or unaware of how to deal positively with the issue? Are they going to be able to advise properly or are they going to tell the thief that what they are doing is wrong and they should simply be punished for it? Or are you going to leave it open for your group to come to their own conclusions?

You answer one question and several other options with other characters open up. Role play can start you on your way as it develops things further. Maybe the thief was bullied prior to their career in stealing. Perhaps being a victim is ongoing for them as they are dyslexic and go to a 'different' school. Maybe they have plus points such as they are good with their hands or very artistic. They are only not able to conform, not able to fit in. Maybe they're nothing of the sort and just jealous of other's apparent wealth and therefore greedy. Your 'actor' must have a picture to perform in their r play because they have a character to act out in a situation with another person a different character and a different viewpoint. They need something strong and complete to hold onto. You are heading for a conflict; a drama; questions.

What is the problem or what are the topics to use? It does depend upon your group, as any dilemma or conflict can be the dramatic subject of your role play. For example: police arrest; divorce; your uncle's confession! Here we have chosen a stereotypical example of a problem. How we choose another is equally important. Start with *what the dilemma is* and you can't go too wrong.

Once you have your dilemma you will wish to contextualise it. In our stealing scenario it was the fifth week of a youth club programme **(when)** in a thief's **(who)** career. Let's use that conflict now as an example. Let's make it Alison **(who)** who's been stealing. Jane **(who)**, her best friend, is the one who knows. The whole club **(where)** is to be punished if the thief is not found out. What should Jane do? We have four characters (Jean, Alison, the youth leader and the shopkeeper) to be established and both where (the youth club) and the when (week 5) are there too. However, we don't have enough information. If you answer the following questions here, then at the end you will be able to start your first role play. Remember: This is a creative process—**invent the answers**.

The character card would be partly or wholly filled in by you and then the rest filled in by your 'actor' or just given to them. You are then throwing them into the scenario with knowledge.

Once each individual character's view point is established in your own mind you are now left with the question of what next? Create scenes which you may or may not ask your group to dramatise. I normally list them and pick my options from them. A quick ten scenes could be:

1. Jean confronts Alison about her stealing before/after the shopkeeper complains.
2. The shopkeeper questions Jean and Alison before/after confronting the youth leader.
3. Alison is confronted by the youth leader after the shopkeeper describes her.
4. The shopkeeper approaches the youth leader to complain.
5. Alison admits all to Jean and explains why before/after the shopkeeper complains.
6. Jean tells on Alison to the youth leader after the shopkeeper complains.
7. The shopkeeper catches Alison in week 6.
8. Alison convinces Jean to join in, in week 6.
9. Jean is caught by the shopkeeper but Alison escapes in week 6.
10. The youth leader denies that anyone could have stolen anything to the shopkeeper.

This does lead you into the question about what the dilemma is designed to prove or reveal and steers you into the realm of stating where you fall in favouring one option or another. Your directing of the role play is therefore significant. With four characters you have nine combinations of individuals but several combinations of opinion and infinite options for creativity.

You can photocopy the blanks (character cards and scenes to be done) and fill them in for each new character.

8-12

1. Alison

Character card:

Alison is ______________ years old. She has a best friend Jean and goes to ______________________ youth club where ________________ is the youth leader. Alison steals from the local shop because ______________________________
Alison has not told anyone why because ______________________________
____

Alison has/has not been caught stealing before. Alison is hoping that __________ ____ happens.

1 Why does Alison steal?

____

____

____

____

2 Has she told anyone why?

____

____

____

____

3 Has she ever been caught stealing before?

____

____

____

____

4 What would be the best thing to happen to Alison?

____

____

____

____

2. Jean

Character card:

Jean is ________ years old. She has a best friend Alison whom she knows is stealing. She goes to the ______________ Youth Club where ____________ is the youth leader. Jean believes Alison steals because ______________
____

Jean has/has not spoken to Alison about it.
Jean is/is not very close to Alison lately.
Jean is prepared to ____

1 Does Jean know why Alison steals?

____
____
____
____

2 Has Jean tackled her about this?

____
____
____
____

3 How close is Jean to Alison?

____
____
____
____

4 Is Jean prepared to lose Alison's friendship by telling on her?

____
____
____
____

3. Youth Leader

Character card:

______________ is the youth leader at the youth club Jean and Alison attend. They have has been approached by ______________ a local shopkeeper who has complained that members of the youth club have been stealing from their shop. ______________ feels that thieves should be ______________ and has known Jean and Alison for ______________. They have has seen the latest project report which mentions Jean and Alison by name. It says ______________. The youth leader has decided that they will ______________.

---

1 How sympathetic is the youth leader and what type of youth leader are they?

____

____

____

____

2 Do they know Alison or Jean well?

____

____

____

____

3 In front of them is the latest project report which tells them about their enthusiasm for the group's activities. What does it tell the youth leader about these two?

____

____

____

____

4 What options after the interviews does the youth leader have?

____

____

____

____

4. The Shopkeeper

Character card:

The shopkeeper has had things stolen every week for five weeks so therefore is more than a little annoyed. They have decided that the best course of action would be to approach those in charge at the youth club.
The shopkeeper has had things stolen so feels ____________________.
They have seen both Alison and Jean before and think ____________________ about them. Their shop doesn't depend/depends on the youth club buying from the shop. The shopkeeper thinks thieves should ____________________.

---

1 How sympathetic is the shopkeeper?

____

____

____

____

2 Do they know Alison or Jean well?

____

____

____

____

3 How much does the shop depend upon members of the youth club buying from the shop?

____

____

____

____

4 What options does the shopkeeper have?

____

____

____

____

N.B. Theft is plagiarism; artistic theft—inspiration!

Preparations for Role Play

Dilemma

Who?

The victim ______________________________

The protagonist ______________________________

The authority figure ______________________________

What? ______________________________

Where? ______________________________

Why? ______________________________

When? ______________________________

Questions to Consider

1 ______________________________

2 ______________________________

3 ______________________________

4 ______________________________

5 ______________________________

6 ______________________________

7 ______________________________

8 ______________________________

9 ______________________________

10 ______________________________

Character cards

Character card:

The story-line for this character

The questions which this character must consider

1

2

3

4

The Role Plays for this character

1

2

3

4

5

Who Are the People to Use—Back to the Who?

In the role plays we moved from situations to characters breathlessly. As continually expressed role play is individual based so make your characters crisp and clean to begin with and then work on them redrafting and redrawing. Try not to stifle your characters. Each member of your group will get a character card. The dilemma can then be told to them and those cards can be filled out by you or them. Some options for development from Jean and Alison's dilemma could be:

Alison may have had a sick mother with no father at home. She was stealing only from supermarkets to feed them both until she saw the £20 note sticking out the shopkeeper's till. Unfortunately a previous conviction for theft of money from a neighbour's house is one of Alison's recent exploits. The youth leader is under threat as her/his youth club is one which may be forced to close due to cuts in local authority services. Their line manager has them under great pressure and a great deal is being placed on the outcome of their investigations. The youth leader needs a result. Will Jean crack?

Again we can invent any character to go with our role play and by asking fairly obvious questions we work up to a situation that now opens up not only the scene in the youth club when the shopkeeper complains but also scenes between Alison and Jean. Did Jean tell? Will Jean confront Alison? Morally, where do you stand?

The Format

Now you're heartily fed up with sorting out the detail it's time to lay it on your group. You have all your information for each character on separate sheets. You describe the situation yourself verbally but not in detail. Have a written sheet for yourself as reference. Give each character their own character sheet without letting them see the other's sheets. Then split them up, give them a role play chosen from your list and let them get on with it!

It is with the basic tools of *who*, *what*, *where*, *why* and *when* that you have created your role play. You have worked towards a solution. Brecht took an entire essay to teach how one incident, an accident, can have many witnesses. These witnesses bring many viewpoints of one historical fact. To take on board Brecht's teaching for a moment helps an understanding of how role play needs the actor to understand their part. Their 'interplay'/'interaction' is where the scenario and dilemma are explored. The dilemma may be solved or merely highlighted but will always raise questions.

Now you've done the spade work all they have to do is make your garden look rosy! Let's recap how did we do it?

- We need a dilemma. **(What?)**
- We need the situation that illustrates our dilemma. **(Where)**
- We need the characters to inhabit the illustration. **(Who?)**
- Who, what, where leaves why and when!

Once they have spent time working on the role play bring them back together as a whole group and ask each group to produce the scene or report back!

ACT ONE, SCENE 4
IMPROVISATION
Now Welcome the Father of Invention

Improvisation

The second type of experience most people readily associate with drama is improvisation. Popularised by *Whose Line Is It Anyway?* the concept of improvisation is simple. You give a totally unprepared group a topic which they then perform around. Their script is unwritten; their performance instantaneous. Whilst you cannot prepare for a random topic being thrown at you, you can prepare yourself or your group on what to do once you are given the topic. As a workshop leader you will be able to prepare your group for dealing with improvisation. How? By practice.

The major difference between role play and improvisation comes in the detail required in preparation for each session. Improvisation should respond to the needs of the group rather than the leader. Improvisation therefore ought to be driven on not by the leader or the 'dramatist' but by the group. It is for this reason that improvisation is better used by people who are comfortable with open ended sessions or after you've been working with drama or your group for a while. It is not for the uninitiated as it takes some understanding of the creative spirit as well as the form to be used. It needs little forethought as there will be no lack of imagination from the group (honestly).

Improvising in a Workshop as Part of the Theatre Techniques

To improvise is 'to perform or make quickly from materials and sources available, with previous planning' or ' to perform as one goes along'. I can't explain it any better than making it up as you go along. This doesn't mean though that you turn up at a group without anything prepared hoping that someone may come up with an idea of what everyone should do—at least not at first!

You can start improvising in a workshop by using a series of games (what a surprise). There are quite a few now well-known thanks to *Whose Line Is It Anyway?* which involve simple props or situations. The following examples are good as starters and can be used as games:

Start line: Beginning with a well-known phrase or saying or sheer gobbledegook you can provide groups of two with a simple beginning for their improvisation. Give groups of two the first line and whoever says it first, has one less line to think of! Examples include:

- Is this your beetle?
- Why is your elephant in my front garden?

- A stitch in time, as you know, saves time.
- Never a borrower nor a lender be.

Party quirks: One person is preparing for a party when their guests arrive, each of whom have an ailment/quirk. The party giver must guess what each quirk is. Prepare easy quirks to begin with like:

- A double glazing salesman.
- A policeman who is looking for a thief.
- A teacher who can't stop criticising.
- A gorilla.

Take it back: In groups of two, one has bought an item recently from their partner. The situation happens when the buyer returns the item, now broken, to the seller to try and gain some form of recompense. The buyer is wanting an exchange or a refund. The seller wishes to give away nothing. Typical examples include:

- The broken walkman which chews tapes.
- The car that falls apart.
- The jumper with sleeves sewn up.
- The trousers with no pockets.

The toe in the bath: One of my favourites. Groups of three. One has a bath in the morning whilst their flatmate is getting up. The person taking the bath gets their toe stuck in the tap and calls their flatmate who finds the situation extremely funny. The flatmate is eventually persuaded to call the plumber. When the plumber arrives, they must solve the problem of the toe in the bath! Each group should take the situation and work towards their own solution. You can then get the groups to perform or simply tell what they did to solve the problem. Two twists are:

1. If they cut the tap off without switching off the water they now have an indoor fountain and
2. The bather has welcomed a complete stranger into their bathroom—did they ask for a towel?

Improvisation as a Performance Piece

The best form of improvisation in a workshop can come when whole groups take over a problem to find an 'ending' for a story. I have outlined three simple cliff-hanger improvisations for three separate age ranges here. The format is simple—you tell them as much information as contained here and then ask them to go off and finish it. Again they may want to perform the piece or simply report on what they have done. This is a performance piece but with this type of cliff-hanger it is the bridge builder between improvisation as a workshop technique and using it as material to teach performance techniques. You can use this as an introduction to the topic or the topic work itself. I would suggest that if you're going to use a cliff-hanger then you may want to use an improvisation game to introduce the 'concept'.

Should these work with your group then don't stop. You can use folklore, books, well-known stories—local or otherwise—or simply make them up yourself!

The Infant Group (8 and Under)

'Last night wee Jamie was in his bed. He had gone to bed late because it wasn't a school night. Just as he was about to fall asleep he heard a noise at the foot of his bed. He opened one eye and saw a green tail disappear out his room. He got up and followed it to the door and saw the tail disappear downstairs. Jamie was joined by his family (dependent upon number in each group) who tiptoe downstairs with them. They get to the hall and see that green tail disappear out the open front door. They creep to the door and open it and . . .'

Upper Primary (9 to 12 Years)

'McGregor was a man who lived at the side of a loch/lake. McGregor's job was a swordsmith in the village, but found that fewer and fewer people needed swords. This was due to the mythical beast said to live in the lake, the Kelpie. Now the Kelpie was the agent of the devil who could turn themselves into any shape or form. They would trick people into joining them usually when in the form of a horse and trick them onto sitting on their back. Then they would ride as hard as they could into the water with their victim who would drown. The devil took the soul and the Kelpie devoured the flesh. One day McGregor was out walking with villagers/members (again dependent upon group numbers) when a black horse approached them. McGregor took out his sword and with the flat of his blade thumped the horse on its nose. Expecting to be attacked by the horse McGregor was surprised to see the horse look at him, open its mouth and drop something shiny at his feet. McGregor then . . .'

Teenage

'It is a family occasion, it may be a wedding, funeral, christening, birthday or whatever. Everyone is gathering for the function afterwards or the party. Just as people have introduced each other and remembered when they last met uncle Harry/aunt Fran/cousin Bert or whoever announces that . . .'

If you wish to use improvisation in order to create a larger performance piece you need to start with some basics such as cliff-hangers before moving on. When you are ready to move on then here are the very basic elements of a growing process. After many years of work I have incorporated my theories into a diagrammatic format which hopefully helps to explain what happens. The *Improvisation Tree* builds upon the format used with role play and the ideas started with role play can be developed through using the tree.

What follows is my *Improvisation Tree*. You have four basic dramatic roots—**place**, **time**, **language** and **style**. Each will determine how your group's finished *Improvisation Tree* shall look and sound. The gateway between the roots and branches is the subject. Exactly the same type of subject as described earlier under *Role Play*. The branches of improvised drama can then flow from the interaction between leader and group. They are dilemma; scenario; characters; scenes; and dialogues. Their places and relationships to each other are highlighted with a basic diagram and is then illustrated with examples of how it is used.

Improvisation Tree

The obviously dramatic which are thought of almost automatically.

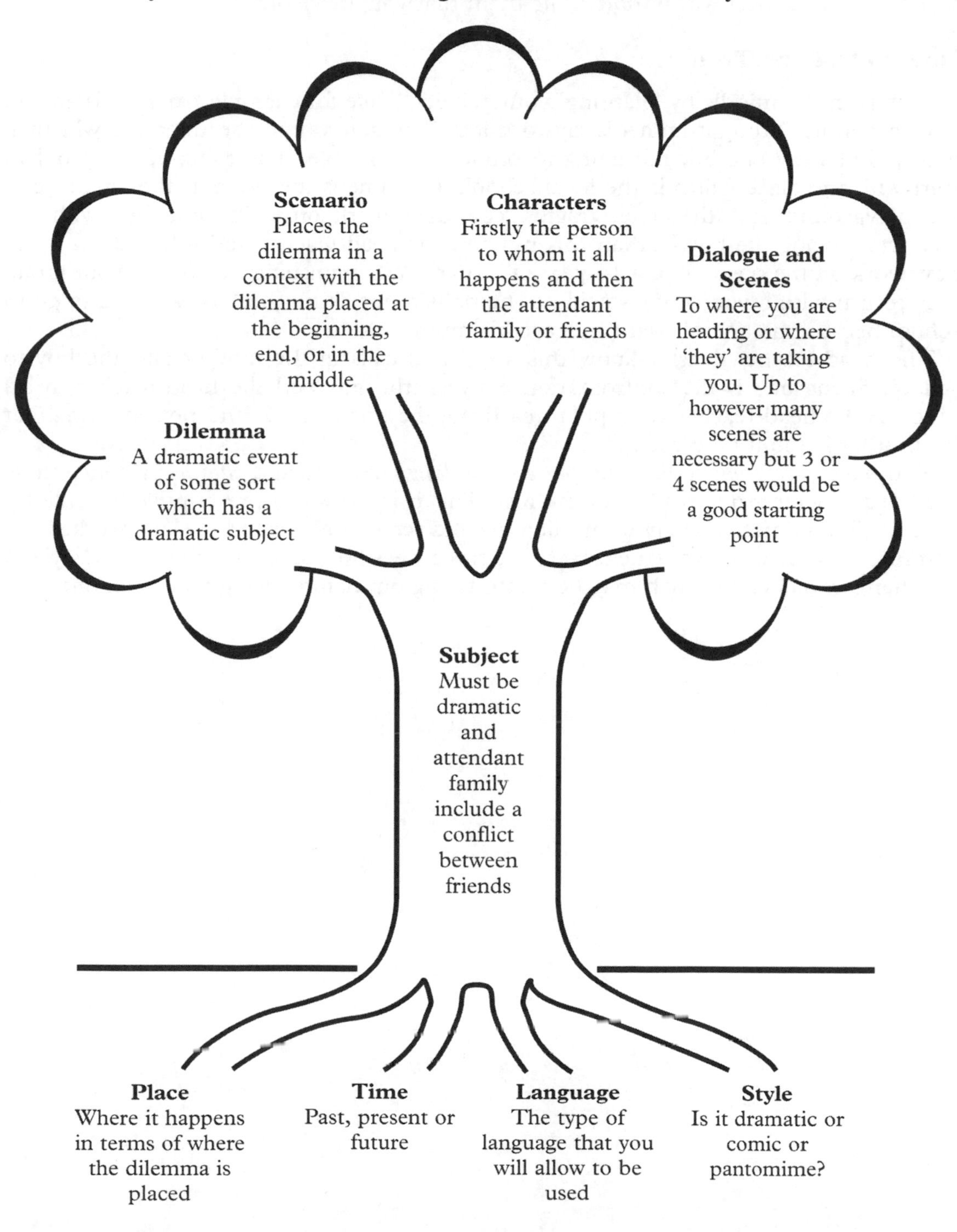

The least obvious considerations but nevertheless very important, particularly language as this about communication. Who are your audience? What are you trying to say? What is the best way of *convincing* them that you are right?

How to Use the Tree

You start in the middle by 'planting' your subject. Take for example truancy. It should have a conflict brought immediately to mind. The gateway to the dilemma will then follow. Let's say one boy not going to school is in trouble. The roots of the problem start with the place which is the local school. The time is the present, the language of the playground and the style, tragic. You then work on your branches with the characters being the boy, perhaps his mother, the head-teacher and a friend. You can now work on the scenario of a 14-year old truant. When pushing this out to your group they return with a young boy staying at home with a sick mother not wanting to go to school because he doesn't want to leave his mum.

The head-teacher doesn't know this at all and calls in the mother and the boy to school. Scene one is the confrontation between the boy and the head-teacher in his office as the head-teacher attempts to castigate the boy as a liar and not believing that his mother is too ill to come in.

You have your *subject*, *dilemma*, *place*, *time*, *language*, *style* and *characters*. Once these are filled in your group works out the rest. This is in no way a prescriptive formula for success. Sometimes you may want dilemma and scenes only or to have one worked out completely in case you get stuck. Here are three trees for you to work on in the style of cliff-hangers as before which may be worth trying out before trying your own one.

The Right To Be Safe

Improvisation Tree

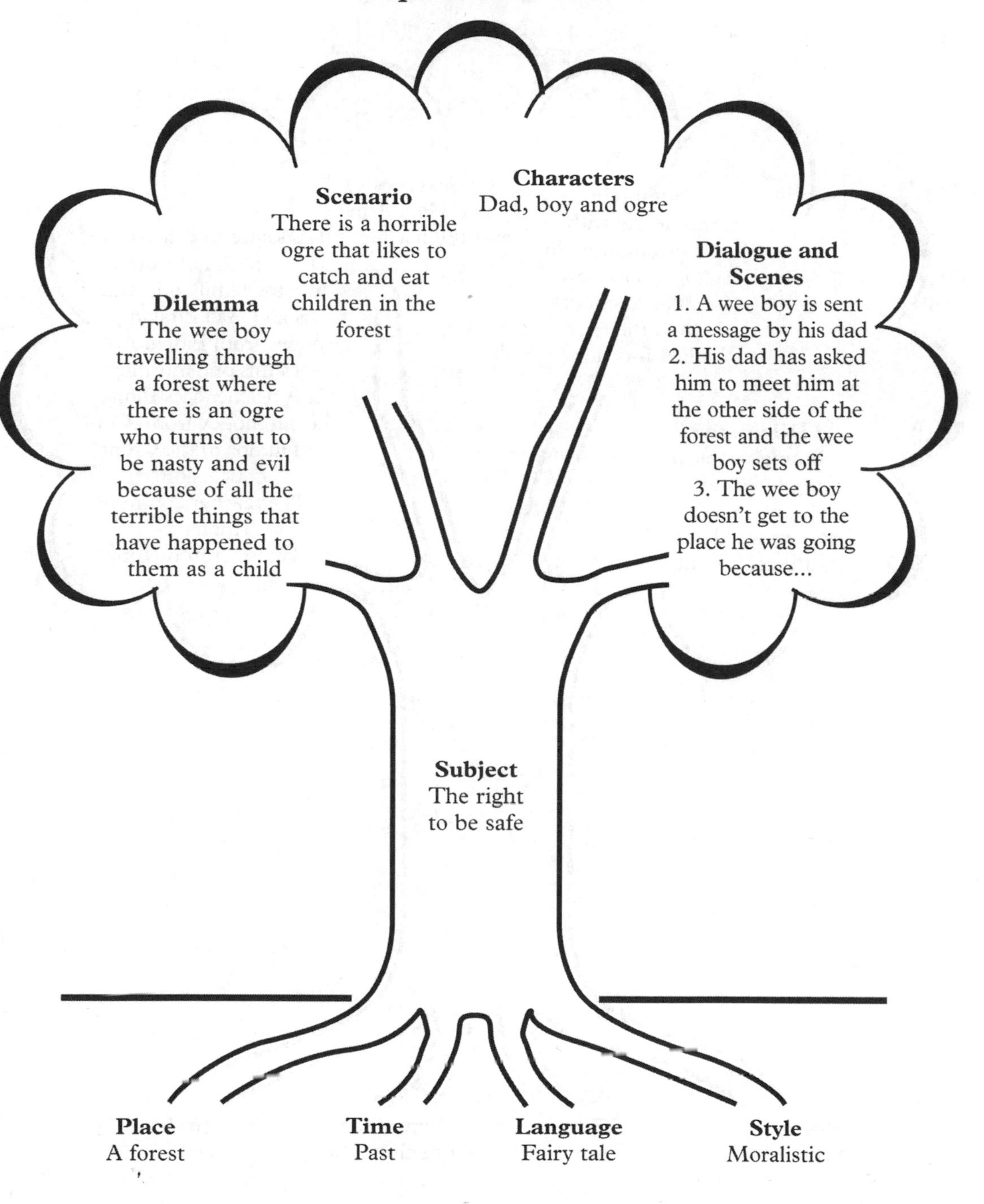

Problem Solving

Improvisation Tree

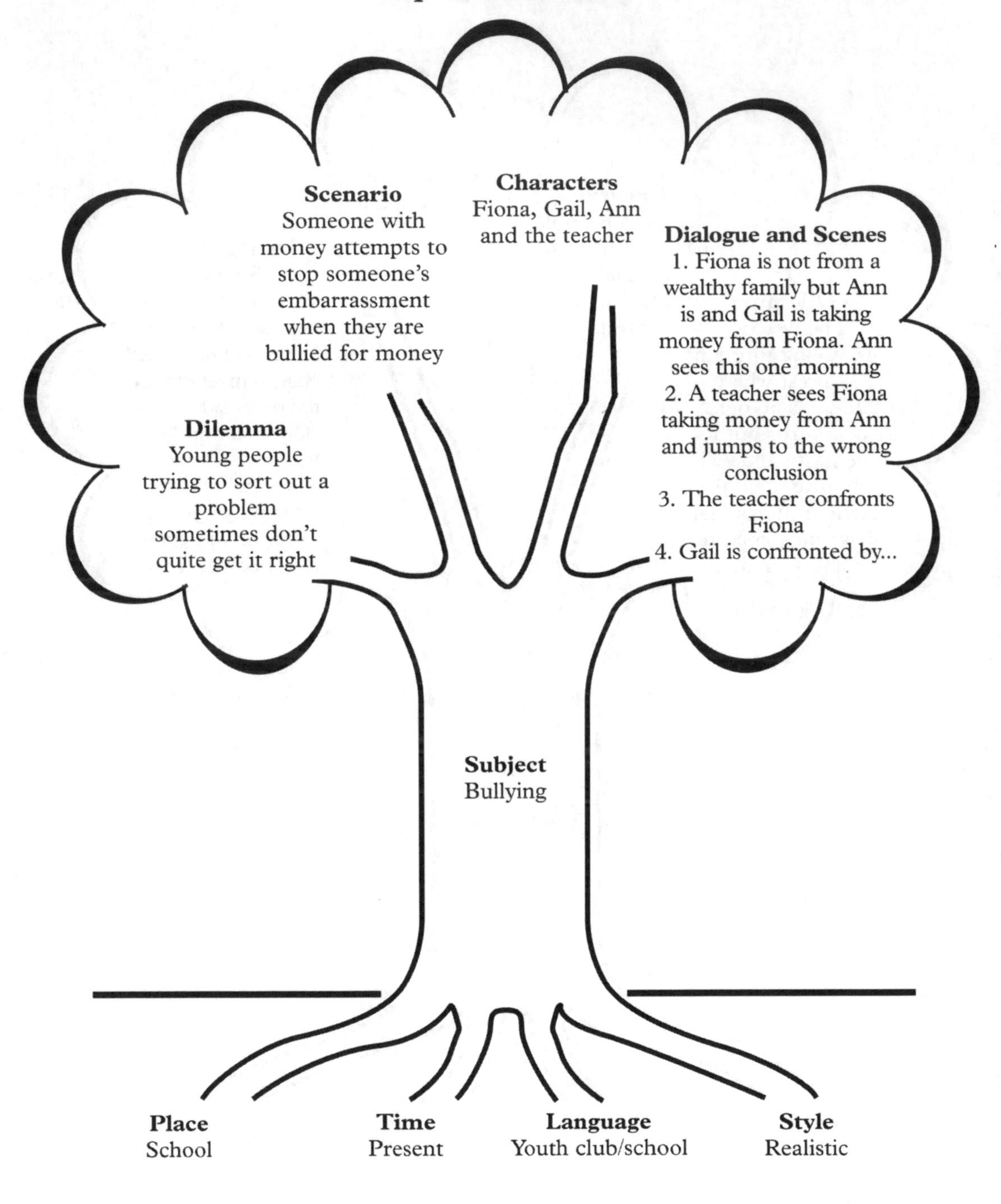

Drugs in the Class—The Problem of How to Help

Improvisation Tree

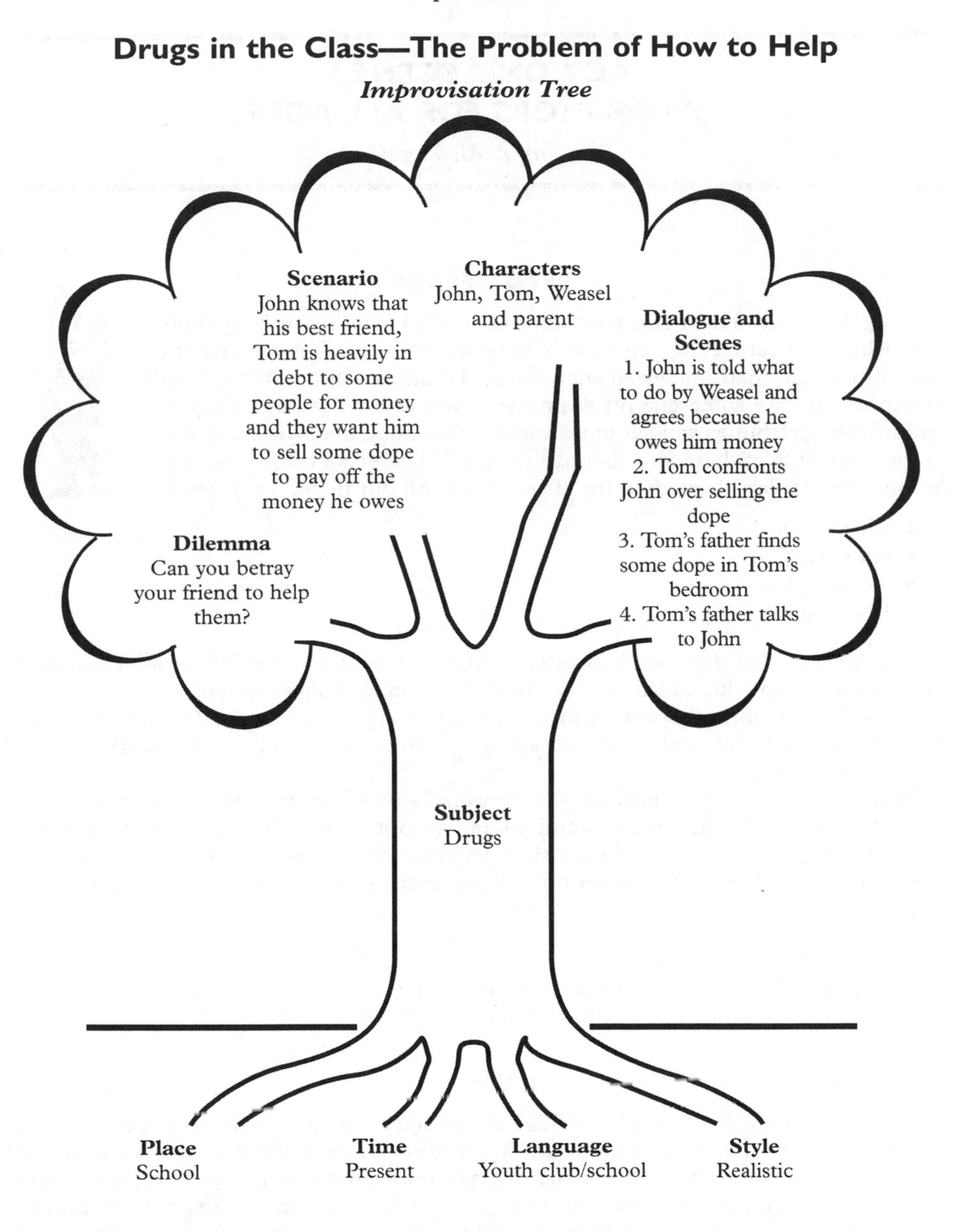

ACT ONE, SCENE 5
WORKSHOPS FOR ALL AGES
Bringing it All Together

Workshops

Having described some of the elements of a workshop let's now look at how and where the various aspects described fit within them. It is important to remember that, there are few, if any, standard drama practices. What I shall describe here are some one-off drama experiences for a group. They are grouped by age but as you get more comfortable using them you may want to use elements of these for other age ranges. If we return to our structure as outlined earlier I have used the structures to fill out these. They were:

- Warm-ups.
- Games.
- Techniques.
- End Games.

The timescale of these workshops is around one to two hours. Be sensitive however to the the group with which you are working. Younger ones will concentrate for less time than older ones. Remember this is merely a guide to topic based workshops. The format is there to be used again and again to produce new and exciting workshops of your own making.

Before I start looking specifically at the workshops I want to place the work in some sort of context. Of course it can stand on its own but to make it truly work, to increase its focus and impact we should consider its relevance in three areas. If you consider these areas first then it shall be purposeful rather than aimless. We want to think about it through:

- It's place in youth work.
- The philosophy involved in its implementation.
- The practice and its dovetailing with existing work.

The Workshop—Its Place in Youth Work

Start with *who is it for*? Begin by looking at the age range and abilities of your group. I would first of all ask the question—*are they theatre interested*? Over the years I have got more and more into trouble by asking this question. There are many people who think that it doesn't matter whether or not your group want to become actors or not—theatre is an enriching, enlivening experience to which they shall warm instantly. Seems a bit naive to me. I mean I believe too that theatre is an enlivening, enriching experience but I wouldn't walk into a young offenders' group and ask them to do a vocal warm-up.

Why? Because that's not why they're there. Their 'interest' may have been forced by their social worker or their supervision order and they may not want to be there. However if you put them at their ease by gently introducing them to drama you will manage to enrich and enliven. Stand them in a circle and ask them to wiggle their fingers and you may be lucky to escape with your own fingers intact.

However the same age group all wanting to do *Twelfth Night* need the discipline of warming up, physically and vocally and you'll need exercises to do that. There is a different approach for each. Therefore if they are there for theatre then yes—the warm-ups would be used; if not leave them out.

The next question to ask would be *what is their attention span*? In challenging groups the span for *some* kids is too short to last longer than say 40 minutes or an hour. It may be lengthened however by putting in a break mid-way.

Now after having considered their age/ability and attention span I would consider your *subject* and *dilemma*. If a youth group is tackling drugs then the subject is drugs! If it's a much younger group, you may wish to choose a more suitable subject matter!

Finally ask yourself *why you are doing it*? If it is to introduce drama to a group not used to drama then perhaps you shall slant the workshop towards theatre interested games and workshop techniques rather than a full-scale 'drama workshop'. If it is to tackle a particular dilemma using drama then your emphasis should be less drama centred and more subject concentrated.

The Philosophy Involved in its Implementation

You may need to decide what your outcome of work will be. Is it a performance or just a workshop? You will also want to work out what your role should be in the session. You can:

Be a 'teacher'. You are out with the drama, directing what happens and therefore have little influence over the content but direct the agenda and affect the outcome.

Be a 'participant'. You are fully involved, perhaps pitching in with the group with problems to help them achieve the performance or telling of the story. You are therefore likely to directly affect the outcome through the content.

Switch between both. You may wish to move between being the teacher and becoming a help when needed. However if more than one group needs help you may need to switch between both roles constantly.

Be an 'actor'. You become directly directed by your group and more dramatically entwined in what is happening.

The role you take on should settle and instruct the young people with whom you are working. Therefore be aware of what you can do or decide what you would like to do and work towards it. However you must be prepared to change if you need to.

You then ask yourself what are your aims—*what you want your group to do*?—and objectives—what you want to be done by the end of the session? If you can—write them down.

The Practice and its Dovetailing with Existing Work

The workshop itself is split into its distinct areas. They are interchangeable and areas can be missed out if felt inappropriate as we've discovered.

Quickly before we delve into them, here's a reminder of the four areas.

Warm-ups

Like an athlete preparing to perform on the athletic field, an actor requires to warm up prior to taking the stage. In recent years it has been fashionable to knock this method of preparation and many companies see actors arrive, dress and perform without any preparation. The advent of much work in television and film also has aided to this lessening of 'craft'.

However the need, prior to walking onstage, to prepare oneself physically, vocally and mentally remains highly important. If you allow yourself to change from yourself to another person, to adopt a new role, how can you achieve that without being ready? How can you project far enough to reach the back of the theatre without a warmed up and fully prepared set of vocal chords? How can you concentrate on the false, within the true to present the fiction to the real?

Within workshops we, therefore, present warm-ups as an example of how preparation is so important to the craft of acting. We introduce the idea of physical warm up which loosens the muscles and makes them more supple and stretchy. These muscles help us adopt the correct posture for our voice which can be used to best effect when our minds are ready to concentrate on the task in hand.

Again we may find ourselves with a group not wanting to perform or who don't want to learn this discipline. We usually miss it out or find a different way of introducing it so that people do the work without realising it. We therefore have a few exercises designed to help you do that.

Physical

Standing in a circle or in front of you warming up a body from fingers to wrists to arms to shoulders to neck to stomach to stretch exercises to running on the spot. Complete warm-ups are running games like touching all four walls and coming back to the circle or games of tig.

Vocal

A specialist area which should be approached with some caution. Only theatre interested groups take to them because they can be repetitive and therefore 'boring'. One simple vocal exercise would be to sing in the round *Frère Jacques* or a similar simple rhyme. Particularly popular are exotic rhymes like Swahili poetry or Yiddish verses.

Mental

Concentration exercises are designed to exercise the imagination whilst at the same time increase an individual's time for which they are able to concentrate. We tend to relax whilst lying on the floor, and just wander through a forest or away for a swim in a lake or wherever they or you feel you want to go by asking them to imagine being there.

Theatre games

Generally we would round off the warm-ups with a game. I usually try to include up to three and connect them by content on theory.

Theatre Technique

As part of the workshop you may want to use a theatrical technique and you may want to introduce it to your group before starting on the technique work in the workshop. For example the bad clown workshop needs you to create a clown! I have described so far role play and improvisation which in the context of youth work may well be enough. I have in the next few workshops included some other theatrical techniques which you can explore or just ignore.

End Games

We want to end on something and round things off—sometimes. I like leaving the group with a feeling of wanting more but some do respond better to endings. It will depend on whether you want your group to leave 'high' or settled as to which type of end game you'll choose. That is if you want to have an end game. Trying to get seven performances from your seven improvisation groups in a two-hour workshop can be very difficult if you want to use an end game. There again your seven performances may turn out to be seven extremely shy groups who don't want to perform but just whisper it in your ear. You then may be glad that you had two or three end games prepared to round off the session!

N.B.: Topic Work: Whatever you are doing drama for, if it is part of youth work, you will usually have a topic to refer to. Your improvisation, role play etc. may extend into this area or may get your group thinking creatively before tackling a topic. The following workshops have very definite topics. We may use improvisation or role play or whatever to look at the topic but the following workshops have definite topics as part of their titles.

The Workshop

Let me remind you of the format that I've used. This is by no means the only format!

Subject

Aims

What do you want the participants to be able to do?

Objectives

What you want to get through.

Workshop

- ***Warm-ups***
  —*Physical*—list of physical exercises.
  —*Vocal*—list of vocal exercises.
  —*Mental*—list of concentration exercises.
- ***Games***
  —List of games to be played.
- ***Techniques***
  —List of techniques you want to cover including role play, improvisation and any other theatre techniques—voice, character, circus and so on.
- ***End games***
  —Games on which to end.

- Any other relevant information, e.g. a topic was done in a story format but what was most interesting was x, y or z.
- Also how they performed i.e. in a ring/if did they perform at all?

N.B. There are three types of workshop which follow. The first were used with five and six-year olds and are relatively basic in content. The next set were used with slightly older kids and are more theatrically based. The final set are more ambitious in content and aimed at teenage/young adult age range. However you may want to mix/match or rearrange to suit yourself—don't hesitate.

Workshops for Younger Groups

Subject: Trip to the Seashore

Aims

- To visualise and participate in a trip to the seashore.
- To sit and listen to the workshop leader tell a story based on the seaside.
- To participate in a whole group improvisation.

Objectives

To cycle to shore, to make sandcastles, eat lunch, go fishing on a fishing boat and then return home.

Workshop

Warm-ups

Physical—Get all of the children to sit on the floor with knees raised. Ask them to get on a bike and set off on a journey to the seaside. They sit with their hands 'on' handlebars above the knees and pedal using their legs. Which direction they follow depends on which way they 'turn' the handlebars. You take them up a hill, down a hill, round two corners and then arrive at the seashore.
Vocal—as this is aimed at the very young and is mainly action based no vocal warm-up is needed.
Mental—none necessary.

Games

Improvisation in group. You visualise the journey and discuss what they saw when they got there. At the shore get them to put sand in a bucket, make a sandcastle, collect shells etc., decorate the sandcastle and then eat their lunch together. Ask them to discuss what they are eating.

Techniques

Whole group improvisation on an imaginary fishing boat which they have to cross a plank into and row. They then drop anchor and throw nets into the sea. Whilst waiting for fish to swim into the nets you invent a story about the seaside with them. When you finish, pull up the nets and find lots of interesting things in them. You then row back to shore and find your bikes.

End games

Use the return journey on the bikes to get them back home and release any pent up energy.

Subject: Vampire Crazy

Aims

- To visualise and participate in a trip to an old castle.
- To sit and listen to the workshop leader tell a scary story.
- To participate in a whole group improvisation.

Objectives

To cycle to the castle, explore the grounds, listen to the story and then disappear as if by magic back home.

Workshop

Warm-ups

Physical—by now, if done as a series, the group shall be well used to the warm-up on the bike. Whilst some warm-ups using the bike may work them physically this warm-up will want to exercise their experiential emotions. You want them to cycle as if scared or not very sure etc.
Vocal—no vocal warm-up required.
Mental—none required.

Games

On arriving at the castle take them exploring the grounds. Get them to look at the headstones and compare how each one died before sitting down to lunch. The game is, as usual, for this type of workshop a prelude to the story and whole group improvisation.

Techniques

Whole group improvisation where they are interrupted by a vampire bat which is found in the workshop leader's pocket. The bat takes them round the castle until they are put in the dungeons. In the dungeons they find a cauldron and gather together ingredients to put in the cauldron. Whilst waiting for the cauldron to boil the workshop leader tells them a very scary story which ends as the cauldron bubbles and bat disappears. The children magically appear back from whence they came as the cauldron's potion has magic travelling properties.

End games

None required.

Subject: Pirate Ship

Aims

- To visualise and participate in a trip on a pirate ship.
- To sit and listen to the workshop leader tell a story.
- To participate in a whole group improvisation.

Objectives

To cycle to the harbour, row to the ship, explore the ship, set sail and then come back to harbour before returning home.

Workshop

Warm-ups
Physical—same route to the harbour as the seashore although slightly different destination.
Vocal—no need for a vocal warm-up although you might want to include a 'sea shanty' when on the boat.
Mental—no mental warm-up.

Games
On arrival at the harbour, before setting off on the rowing boat you need to get everything packed on the boat which you need for the day. You then row together before getting on board and exploring the boat so you unpack, the anchor snaps and you begin to float.

Techniques
Whole group improvisation where the children then have to stop the ship from drifting. They have to learn all about hoisting a sail by pulling together on a rope and then navigating together past some rocks before the spare anchor is found just before you crash into the harbour walls! Once you're at anchor play a quick game of port/starboard. Then have them improvise a pirate story. You no longer need the rowing boat as you are next to the harbour. So it's a nice walk across the plank.

End games
The bike ride home.

Workshops for Middle Ages!

Subject: Character Building

Aims

- To allow children to explore inventing a new person.
- To demonstrate how to keep that person going over a sustained period of time.

Objectives

To create several characters and play them in a variety of settings.

Workshop

Warm-ups
Physical—full physical warm-up through three games of physical tig.
Vocal—full vocal warm-up—humming, aahs, breathing.
Mental—none required.

Games
Stock character game which involves asking them to walk about the room as: yourself; a young person; an old person; an astronaut; a joiner; someone who is frightened; someone who is brave; someone you want to be.

Techniques
Improvisations using one of the characters that they have created. A simple improvisation in pairs involving an interview for a job. You then ask various members of the group to show examples of each character—the young, the old, the astronaut, the joiner, the brave person and the frightened person—you want to focus on the characteristics of their caricatures. Once you have discussed them you focus on the old person. Show them how to behave in character by creating an old person individually getting them to make tea. After that exercise, ask them to walk with ankles getting stiff then knees, then hips, then back bending and sore shoulders. Talk through the exercise before the improvisation *Who Stole the Sugar?*

In an old folks home it is mid-morning and teatime. The four old people come into the old folk's home sitting room for tea. One by one they find that there is no sugar. Someone has stolen it but which one of these 70(+)-year olds was it? Discuss each character—their age, type of voice, family and who's left and tea/coffee after they've finished the improvisation. Then ask them to walk round the room and talk outside of their groups to create a relationship with other characters. After that they report back as their character about any other characters they have just met. They then are hot spotted where we put each under a 'spotlight' and everyone can ask them questions, any questions within reason, about their characters before going into a group and creating a short scene involving a queue at a bus stop.

End games
Again you may want to relieve the hard cerebral work having been done with a physical game like the *bear and the honeypot.*

Subject: Clowning

Aims

- To invent a clown routine involving a bad clown.
- To understand the elements involved in clowning.

Objectives

To create a clown character with voice and walk and then interact with three other group members in an improvised routine.

Workshop

Warm-ups
Physical—full physical warm-up whether three games of tig or in circle from fingers to toes.
Vocal—no vocal warm-up necessary as we're working in mime.
Mental—no mental warm-up required because we're working **big**.

Games
We want to play a mime game like *Chinese mime whispers*.

Techniques
Children think up a clown name, then one by one must come out and shout it out to the rest of the group. On each occasion everyone must applaud them. They then do the same by giving their clown a walk which they must keep. Finally the same again, name

and walk and whether they're happy or sad. You now divide them into groups of 4–5. In each group one must be the bad clown. No matter what the clowns are trying to do—fix something or perform a basic rescue or whatever—the bad clown will trip them up, get it wrong or just get in the way. Once they have rehearsed their routine it's show time! Each group will then perform their piece with mats for the more adventurous if necessary.

End games

A mental ring game like *the minister's cat* usually calms them back down.

Workshops for the Older Groups

In 1996 I was approached by the social work department in South Ayrshire to prepare and produce eight weeks of workshops for a throughcare project working with young people who had recently left the 'care' system.

The project titles of each workshop were:

Week	Format and Focus
One	Whole group improvisation
Two	Dealing with authority
Three	Dealing with authority II
Four	Forward with confidence
Five	Forward with confidence II
Six	Communicating with each other
Seven	Socially acceptable
Eight	Authority v socially acceptable behaviour

The workshop headings were by necessity very vague as the group dictated the type of workshop to be produced, however there has to be some form of basic structure.

Aims

The aims of the eight weeks were twofold. Firstly there was the need to build up the group in terms of its involvement and use of drama. Secondly there was a need to impart to the leaders how to use drama to encourage members of the group to deal with their own situations with confidence and authority.

Objectives

The objectives, drawn from the aims were:

- An 8 week programme rolling through dealing with authority; working with confidence; social cohesion and communication for the benefit of the group.
- The drama specialist's role would be to work with the group then work with the leaders to establish a drama format.

Background

The group started with no understanding of drama or how to perform it. They had attended a group run by the Social Work Department which was 'self help' oriented. I was about to become a bit of a culture shock. Therefore I started with basics. The most basic starting point is that we all have a story to tell. Within vulnerable groups we need to develop a way of exploring their issues without exposing them to ridicule or Oprah Winfrey style inspection. The way in which we do this is by fictionalising a life or 'packaging a story'. Prior to embarking on this I started by exploding myths about drama. What follows covers **all** the work we did. It shows both methodology and result. If you have problems with the methodology then just use the results as a basis for a workshop with older kids.

Workshop

Warm-ups—None.

Games—None.

Techniques

Bring in the idea of familial breakdown and problems. Demonstrate 'how' to put together a drama and move on to acting it out. Plan a story about a family. Then draw up a family tree like the one below.

N.B. I was working with a group which had no experience of drama, run by the Social Work Department. To lesson the culture shock we talked on the basics. What was immediately complex was their story. The skill is to translate the complex story into a simple storyline.

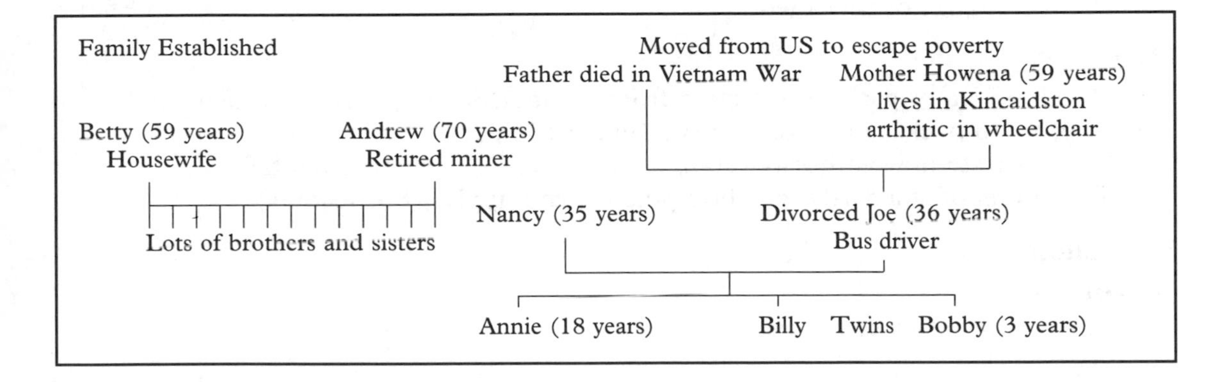

Situation

- Joe and Nancy split two years ago because twins were half-caste and Joe did not believe they were his.
- Two years on Annie is arrested for trying to shoot swans on the River Ayr using her grandfather's old Vietnam pistol

Story-line

Some years later: The time and place

Scene 1: Annie locked in her room at home. She won't come out. Mother, Nancy is extremely worried. Eventually Sharon her best friend talks her out.

Scene 2: Social worker on her way to pick Annie up is harassed as she's late getting the kids to the child minder, has a flat tyre and then finishes with a migraine.

Scene 3: Picking Annie and Nancy up she has a big argument with them on the way to court. Annie slams doors shut.

Scene 5: Outside the court, Annie sees how scary the whole place is, runs to the toilet, locks herself in and cries.

Scene 5: At the hearing Annie receives a 41(B) and is sent for assessment at Newfield.

Scene 6: Annie is shown her room and the door is locked behind her.

The development
Having established a the story-line it is important to introduce an element of 'acting'. This allows you to quicken the impact **and** to demonstrate how easy it is to 'do drama'. You eventually push the piece forward after some discussion.

End games
None

Subject: Dealing with Authority

Aims

Taking it on from the previous week we now needed to build up the group by getting them 'up' to perform. It was also clear that to develop leaders' techniques it was important to involve them in the workshop to demonstrate how the techniques or tricks work.

Objectives

- Develop idea of packaging a story from a 'fantastic' angle. (For participants)
- Apply it to packaging a 'real story'. (For participants)
- Demonstrate how authority rebuffs 'real stories'. (For participants)
- Take parts of standard workshop practice and apply. (For leaders)

Workshop

Warm-ups
Mental—we played *minister's cat.*

Games
None.

Techniques
Storytelling.

Introduce the idea of a superhero in the local town. For us it was Superman, man of steel and great hero but who now has a fault—he isn't quite as goody two shoes as he's made out to be. Landing on Earth and taken in by an elderly Maybole couple Superman begins a dastardly life of crime in South Ayrshire only to be stopped by Super Social Worker Pat.

This was a means to an end. Not designed to be developed—like last time—or performed like next week, it was designed to demonstrate that authority, all authority, has limits. Superman, after all has kryptonite as his limit.

Story
Scene 1: Whilst his adoptive parents are seen out shopping, two elderly people see a falling star which hits the grounds of the Maytag Building. Stunned by his mother

dropping him on the head whilst a baby on planet Krypton, Superman has turned bad. The baby kicks open the door of the spaceship and the elderly woman is captivated by him. The elderly couple decide to keep him.

Scene 2: Whilst out for their pension one day we see Superman in the background robbing the shops Daily Bake and Spar.

Scene 3: The Super Social Worker is on her way to Girvan when held up by thug Superwoman on the zebra crossing. Getting out of her car she takes 'an absolute flaky' and thumps him on his head. Superman is cured through the bump to his head.

Exercises

Talking about this story which demonstrates that superheroes, good or bad, have to be dealt with by 'authority', we moved on to who 'authority' is? We got:

- Teachers
- Social workers
- Police
- Parents
- DSS
- Housing officials
- Head-teachers

As housing is a particular issue for young people we homed in on housing officials. We discussed how to negotiate with their authority. We discovered that a particular problem was having to deal with being cut off whilst owing large sums in back payments for electricity. That became Role Play V and we moved to a participative workshop.

We discovered that going into meetings with a proposed solution worked out in advance helps and despite, in many instances, extreme provocation from that authority the way to deal properly and satisfactorily with authority figures is with:

- Calmness.
- Knowledge.
- Being sure of exactly what you want.

To bring things to a close mix people up and finish on some drama games.

End games

Tell a story.

THE INTERVAL
INTEGRATED WORKSHOPS
A Bridge Between

The Integrated Workshop—An Explanation

The recipe goes like this: Take 20 + children; put them in a room; tell them they're in a village, take them through some days in the life of a village, tell them something terrible is going to happen: kidnap the most popular person in the village using the secret police; tell his wife and children you don't know where he's gone; tell them you hear he was executed. Stop the workshop; then discuss. That is basically an Amnesty workshop!

The local Amnesty group felt it inappropriate for some of their material to be given to the very young. I sympathised but felt we could use allegory or example to explain some of the more hideous torture without going into any detail. After all, that torture is bad wasn't a contentious statement. Describing the use of electrodes may have been too frightening! We decided on using the local Amnesty cause.

Each local Amnesty group adopts a prisoner for whom they campaign. Our local group had a Burmese monk. They checked that it was OK to let us in on his case and were ready to begin six weeks of workshops on his situation. One week before we were due to start the Burmese Government released him. Whilst we were obviously delighted for him it did cause a bit of a problem for us.

I picked up some literature and surveyed some options. There were thousands. Similar tales of woe, horrendous attempts to crush the human spirit. All we needed was to alter the storyline but keep the format and a workshop would develop. There was the key! I stopped panicking and started planning.

The first workshop which we did was indicative of that approach. I have now lost the leaflet which introduced me to the idea but it came from a story, which was was only four sentences long. No more. It launched us into six workshops which lead to eight on the environment and many ideas which are still not completely finished with.

The difference between these workshops and previous ones is that they throw the structure outlined earlier out and move onto complete mini improvised performances with their own new structure. That is why they are the bridge between workshops and performances, for they are two-hour improvised performances in a workshop. The structure they do have is that each group is divided into 'families' who 'live' somewhere. They attend a routine day: breakfast, lunch, dinner, bedtime. You, as workshop leader call out the times and use 5 a.m. as the control time to impart information which is when they sleep. In between calling out times you will wander around talking to various participants asking them, at prearranged times to make an event happen. Only the workshop leader will know their connections or how the thing should develop. The 'happening' will come after the world in which the characters inhabit is well established.

The 'happening' will often shatter the world the participants have created. Their personal investment shall underpin their view of it and thus enrich, enliven and focus debate at the end.

With the environmental workshops we extended that theory into a programme of eight weeks. The programme developed an imaginary village that by week eight was environmentally unviable. It was left to pick ten notable citizens to survive the holocaust leaving the rest of the village to perish. We used this methodology with eight primary schools over a smaller four-week period. Their response to each crisis we wrote into the environmental play *Global Warning* which then toured round schools. Because of the impact and immediacy of the workshops the material in the play became highly accessible for the audiences. I've not included this development here but I am sure there are many issues which could benefit from the same type of treatments as the Amnesty and environmental issues explored here.

Workshop One—The School Experience

Subject
Freedom of expression.

Scenario
Scots is banned from being used in school.

Characters
1. Head-teacher.
2. Two security guards.
3. Two pupils who object.
4. Teachers.
5. Pupils.
6. Parents.

Dialogue and Scenes
Five days at a school in the life of a school.

Dilemma
Parents at a local school are upset that their children are speaking in a dialect which is not the Queen's English. They badger the head-teacher to ban the use of the dialect.

Place
A school.

Time
Present.

Language
Mixture of 'dialect' and proper English.

Style
Realistic.

N.B. Before starting you may want to identify in your own group who the characters will be played by. You can then pick on them on the appropriate days as they develop your plot. If you have a small 'team' then your 'team' will be the principal characters. I developed this idea further in 1998 when I was asked to undertake consultation work with young people. I used our young people within these workshops as a basis for that work. The consultations were to be used to create the Council's Children's Service Plans required under the Children (Scotland) Act 1995. I used the format and brought in the story of the *Pied Piper of Hamlyn* creating a corrupt council who could therefore be challenged and changed by the workshop participants, thus creating their personal view of the services and a plan of a fictional council. This allegory allowed us to produce critical yet sympathetic views of council services. It was therefore an extension, and a fairly practical and exciting extension of the previous work.

The Workshop

The workshop can be started with young people of various ages. Start by warming them up with everyone in a circle. Move on to some improvisation games before splitting them up for the work.

Split the group into families of about four. Allocate sufficient teachers for each class of six to ten pupils, a group of parents, a head-teacher and security guards who patrol the school. The more able split up into the Head-teacher, one of the security guards, one teacher, two pupils and two parents. These groupings come as a layer on top of the family groupings.

Create a village street into which each family is put and then instruct them to go to bed at the beginning, allowing you to explain what is about to happen. The numbers given to each family group represent the numbers on the street.

The Head-teacher is separate, outside of the family groups and lives in another street. N.B. I use the word 'cut' a lot. It means move swiftly to the next bit.

Day one

5.00 a.m. The peaceful time at which everyone is asleep. At this time you are giving out the following information that will see them through the next few 'days'. In the first day you are asking them to think about the character they are about to spend the next two hours playing. They are not encouraged to be the family dog or cat unless they want to spend the next two hours crawling on hands and knees barking or going meeow! In fact I usually ban animals and babies for my own sanity! The leader is the caller of the times and at each time the group must respond by behaving as their character would at that time of the day. At 5 a.m. everyone in the village or street is asleep.

Take a few moments to ask them in their groups to create their characters and their families in their minds. They must think about parents, children, work/school, ages, family and insignificant facts like what they eat for breakfast and whether they drink tea or coffee. Each time you work on a character exercise you can see them develop their ideas further and more excitingly.

7.00 a.m. At this time the family starts to wake up. In various areas there shall be families having their breakfast as well as those wishing to spend their time lazing in bed. We usually have mothers, wherever, making the breakfasts and men trying to stay asleep! Or maybe as a by-product of what we are doing we want to directly challenge it.

8.00 a.m. By now the group shall all be trying to have breakfast. Those more able in groups should attempt to get them to work on the making of the breakfast in real time rather than in ten seconds. The leader should prompt by asking people within groups to comment on the breakfast TV, talk about the day ahead, think about the argument they had last night etc.

9.00 a.m. By now they will have gone through getting those who need to get ready to go to school. You want to have the teachers driving into school and pupils arriving or being dropped off to spend the day there. This is the second quiet time as there is school assembly first thing as it is a Monday and you need to identify people to read out lessons and speak to the class. If you make it a special assembly then the whole community are in for the duration of the assembly. You make one end of the room the school and be prepared to make the other end a factory (it may be old fashioned to have one large employer in the town but it does help to take parents to work for the day).
9.15 a.m. Straight after the assembly the pupils go to their classes, taken by their teachers. Whilst they are in class the more able parent shall be stirring up anti-Scots language slang bias* in a Parents' Association meeting and the head-teacher will be taking his coffee break. It is also necessary for the chosen pupil to identify the person who will stand with them when they are told that their language is to be banned.
10.40 a.m. It is break. The parent's meeting breaks up and the classes go out into the playground. At some point we like to freeze the action and focus in on one group to get others to watch what is going on and perhaps get some ideas. The security guards patrol the playground with the head-teacher. The teachers are off for coffee in the staff room.
11.00 a.m. Back to class and the teachers go back in to teach. The parents have a village life to continue and much selling and buying at a local shop is to be done and that is where the major effort will be going on from the leader's part as you should have a pattern for the school established.
Lunch-time Due to the privatisation of meals all dinners are home dinners so all leave the school to go home. Again there needs to be a lot of encouragement from the leader in terms of prompts that will suggest topics of conversation just as in the morning. By now you will have some gossip from somewhere to drop into the conversation and instructions to allow the participants struggling to participate more fully. Return after lunch-time to school.
2.45 p.m. At this time we have another break from school life to allow the staff back into the staff room and to let them cement relationships. A chosen teacher shall be a very right wing member of staff designed to stir up trouble. After a few minutes back to class. The factory can take a tea break; the pupils depart to the playground.
3.30 p.m. Home time or at least the walk back to the house to await tea. This is the real test time particularly on the first day as there are likely to be real problems if it isn't working. You could end up with 'trouble'. The amount of time that this section takes will depend upon how capable the group are. If they can't hack it, cut it right down for teatime.
Teatime Back to sitting down for a meal with the family and talking over the day's events—who got a punishment exercise for what and who stole what from whom. Again there should be some prompts from the leader to help conversation.
7.00 p.m. The next problem time as you can end up with as much hanging around as when they are coming home from school. Again the leader should assess the tension and cut to suit. We cut straight to 'bedtime' if there are any 'boredom' problems.

**This is particularly an issue in Scotland (and I don't mean Gaelic) we have a third language—Scots. It is seen by those and such as those as 'slang' or 'lazy language' and it is frowned upon. But with a syntax, grammar and beauty it is a language. However in English dialects/local languages can be substituted here.*

Day two

5.00 a.m. The leader should review the previous day by taking them through specific parts to remind them of what happened and also to tell them to watch out for what is about to be set up. The leader should tell them about day two and that there will be a parent's meeting at which every parent should agree with what is suggested.
7.00 a.m. Wake up call.
8.00 a.m. Get ready to go to school.
9.00 a.m. Everyone goes off to class. No assembly this morning. Parent's meeting that morning where the chosen parent deplores the state of the school and complains about the state of the language spoken by some of the pupils.
10.40 a.m. Interval at the school where there is a 'fight' between the chosen pupil and the other person picked by them who shall object to the ban. The security guards separate them and take them to the head-teacher. their punishment is very slight.
11.00 a.m. Back to classes with everyone hopefully talking about the fight. If not prompt them.
Lunch-time Back home for their lunch with news of the fight to spread to the parents. The chosen parent is appalled at such behaviour and there will be a call for a meeting with the head-teacher at the school tomorrow afternoon. Back to school after lunch.
2.45 p.m. The school has its afternoon break and pupils get together to discuss the parents' views as expressed when they were at home for lunch. Back to class and there may be a chance for the teachers to be involved in the discussions.
3.30 p.m. The school goes home and for the first time the security guards are asked to patrol the streets on the way home.
Teatime There should be by now trouble brewing. Again leaders should prompt where there's not. Teatime at each family home is designed to create an atmosphere between parents and pupils.
7.00 p.m. A quick bedtime.

Day three

5.00 a.m. The quiet time where we go back over the days' events. You want to create a sinister feel and up the tension. You also want to inform them that during the next day there will be a parents' meeting.
7.00 a.m. Time to wake up.
8.00 a.m. Getting to school.
9.00 a.m. School and the meeting of parents where they are told that they can't see the head-teacher until tomorrow. Their mood is turning ugly as they think the head-teacher weak and ducking the issue.
10.40 a.m. The school break and yet another fight breaks out between two more pupils. One of the pupils disappears from the school taken by the security guards. You extract them from the workshop and they can either sit out the rest and observe or come back a day later with some frantically lurid tale of where they've been.
11.00 a.m. The classes go back to work.
Lunch-time The news of the morning fight gets home.
2.45 p.m. There are rumours that one of the pupils involved in the fight has been sent to hospital.
3.30 p.m. School gets out and people are watched by the security guards who now are

moving the pupils on home. You pull the more able pupil aside and tell them that during the next day they will form a Scots Language Society and recruit members. If they are told by any teacher that it is to be stopped then they must stand up and argue for their rights.
Teatime The parents are uneasy.
7.00 p.m. Curfew is imposed for the first time.

Day four
5.00 a.m. Go back over the days' events.
7:00 a.m. Wake up.
8.00 a.m. Get to school.
9.00 a.m. The day starts with a parents meeting whilst everyone else is at school. They are adamant that the lawlessness must end and basic discipline must be restored. They decide that the first place to start is by outlawing their filthy Scots language.
10.40 a.m. The break sees an army of parents arriving at the school in big numbers.
11.00 a.m. The chosen pupil sets up their Scots Language Society and starts to recruit new members. Back to class whilst the parents demand the withdrawal of Scots language from the vocabulary of each pupil. There is a special assembly called there and then. We have each of the classes brought into the school assembly hall with their teachers and parents sit directly behind the head-teacher. Before the assembly the security guards must be told that anyone who objects is to be taken forcibly from the room. The head-teacher tells them at this assembly of the ban and two pupils object. The school guards remove them and they are taken out of the workshop. The classes are sent back to their rooms. From now on you are calling out the events and leaving them to react.
Lunch-time Lunch at home.
2.45 p.m. Break at school.
3.30 p.m. End of school day.
Teatime Teatime at home.
7.00 p.m. Curfew.

Day five
5.00 a.m. Recall the days' events and add the rumour that the two pupils have been arrested and sent to prison for creating an anti-authority language society.
7.00 a.m. Wake up.
8.00 a.m. Get to school.
9.00 a.m. School starts.
10.40 a.m. Break.
11.00 a.m. End of break.
Lunch-time Go home.
2.45 p.m. Break the workshop here for discussion on the human rights issues that have been unearthed. You want to discuss and explore their feelings as their characters and you ought to get a reaction that it would never happen here. At or around this point I bring in the Albanian source.

Workshop Two—The Street Children of Brazil

Subject
Right to life.

Scenario
Children are disappearing from a large community made up of children.

Characters
1. Two secret police.
2. Children.

Dialogue and Scenes
Five days in the life of street children.

Dilemma
From an estimated 7,000 homeless street children there have been several 'disappearing'. A small community of children have been untouched until six, aged 9 to 17 were taken and killed or seriously wounded.

Place
The streets.

Time
Present.

Language
Their own.

Style
Realistic.

On 28th November 1991 an estimated 3,000 children marched through the streets of Rio de Janeiro, to protest against the killing of street children. Two weeks earlier six, aged 9 to 17, were killed and a girl was seriously injured in a Rio suburb. The children were reportedly taken from a hut to a field, made to lie down and shot in the head at point blank range.*

We wanted to take the disappearances and create a community out of which they would come. Because of the ages we were working with we did not necessarily want to become involved in the details of six children being murdered. It was something we would, only refer to if they asked.

We approached this in the following way:

- Two members of the youth theatre were extracted early to be the policemen who are feared by everyone each time they appear.
- The whole group was then split into groups of 3 to 4.
- They became family units with a structure.
- None of the families involved adults.

**A parliamentary commission of inquiry reported that over 7,000 homeless children have been murdered between 1987–1991 by death squads, often made up of off duty police officers.*

The Workshop

Day one

5.00 a.m. The peaceful time at which everyone is asleep. At this time you are giving out the information that will see them through the next few 'days'. In the first day you are asking them to think about the character that they are about to spend the next two hours playing. They are **not** as usual encouraged to be the family dog or cat unless they want to spend the next two hours crawling on hands and knees barking or going meeow! You will be the caller of the times and at each time they must respond by behaving as their character would at that time of the day. At 5 a.m. everyone in the community is asleep.

7.00 a.m. At this time the community starts to wake up. In various areas there shall be people looking for and finding their breakfast as well as those wishing to spend their time lazing in makeshift shelters or boxes. You should see young people wherever, making the breakfasts and young boys particularly trying to stay asleep!

8.00 a.m. By now the group shall all be trying to have some sort of breakfast or complaining about about no breakfast at all. You send in the two policemen who begin their first patrol. You want to begin their first day with a shadow over the community.

9.00 a.m. By now you will want to inform them that nobody needs to go to school. They need to find something therefore to occupy their time. What is important is that they connect as characters as well as discerning the mind numbing boredom of days of nothing to do. It's interesting to do this exercise with young people about to leave school with a desire to be 'on the dole'.

11.00 a.m. The dropping off of food at a local hall brings excitement to a dull day. This is particularly so as the hall gives out lunch to the local children; as long as they cook it themselves. Here you are introducing an element of communal co-operation. You may want to see if those who had no breakfast in the morning act any hungrier than those who did!

Lunch-time Due to the children making meals by themselves all of them eat lunch as one community so all have a chance to pass on gossip and talk about what may be happening 'on the outside'. Take aside one and tell them that they've just heard that some children in the nearby village have disappeared. Towards the end of lunch-time the two policemen should come to eat. The community must prepare their meals for them and the atmosphere should change. If you can manage this without having to point it out all the better.

2.45 p.m. After lunch-time it is up to each 'family' to find enough food for dinner time. At this time you want them to come back together probably at the 'hall' for another 'youth council' to talk about issues of the day. They have all managed this time to secretly steal away from the police. It is important, therefore, to get the actors playing the policemen out of the room during this time. It increases the feeling of mutual mistrust.

Teatime This is basically a back to sitting together as a family time, except it's outside and not in the hall. Whilst there is community time there is also family/private time. There is also a great deal of boredom and hunger.

7.00 p.m. The problem with this time is there can be much hanging around as there won't be much to do. The two policemen come and do a final check to sort out a curfew. Again we feel the tension and cut to suit. We cut straight to 'bedtime' as soon as you feel enough has been done.

Day two
5.00 a.m. We review the previous day by taking them through specific parts to remember and also to tell them to watch out for what is about to be set up. All you tell them about day two is that there will be a youth council meeting at which everyone will agree with what is suggested.
7.00 a.m. Wake up call.
8.00 a.m. Get ready to have breakfast, if you've remembered to collect some food on day one!
9.00 a.m. The police 'do their rounds'.
11.00 a.m. Off to prepare for lunch at the community hall. The two policemen do a surprise visit just to check and leave again.
Lunch-time There is now definite news from the neighbouring village that 25 children have been taken away. Rumours are that people in uniform arrive during the night. Just at the height of this commotion send in the two policemen for their lunch.
2.45 p.m. A youth council where one member of the group is given a slip of paper which confirms that the rumours are true. It has been sent from the neighbouring village and the paper asks for support and that all the children from that community march on the streets on Day five.
Teatime The two policemen coming back break up the youth council and everyone nips off to their family groups to eat—if they have any food.
7.00 p.m. The two policemen impose a 7 p.m. curfew and tension should be heightened.

Day three
5.00 a.m. The quiet time where we go back over the days' events. The next day will see an event which will polarise the community. You want to then tell the policemen that next day they will try to take away all the food at the community hall, they should be prepared to compromise if necessary but will have to warn six indviduals to beware. During the next night they will 'lift' those who ought to be six of the weakest characters in the group.
7.00 a.m. Time to wake up.
8.00 a.m. Breakfast?
9.00 a.m. The day begins with the forage for food.
11.00 a.m. Food is dropped off at the community hall and the two policemen arrive to take it away. The ensuing argument sees an uneasy compromise or does it?
Lunch-time Is there any food to eat?
2.45 p.m. There are reports at the youth council that the disappeared children were murdered.
Teatime The two policemen do the rounds and warn the individuals not to be too cocky.
7.00 p.m. Curfew is imposed again. During the night the six are taken. Or at least as many as can be taken. If there is too much resistance take one or two.

Day four
5.00 a.m. Go back over the days' events. They are informed that at any time from now in Day four if you are asked to go, then you will go.

7.00 a.m. Wake up.
8.00 a.m. Breakfast.
9.00 a.m. The police go for a wander.
11.00 a.m. Food arrives at the community hall. The policemen go for their 'share'.
Lunch-time Lunch.
2.45 p.m. Youth council. The missing children are now feared dead.
Teatime Teatime.
7.00 p.m. Curfew.

Day five
5.00 a.m. Recall the days' events and tell them that a bus will arrive at 9 a.m. for the rally.
7.00 a.m. Wake up.
8.00 a.m. Breakfast. The two policemen arrive and stand at the head of the hall. They warn people not to go to the rally.
9.00 a.m. The bus arrives and the policemen remain. How many will go to the rally?

Discuss the events at the end of the workshop. The information you have may inform your 'debate' with the young people. Remember we wish to recreate the feelings and conditions of being in this type of situation. In one workshop we found that the young people started with a fairly futuristic setting because they were not comfortable with the idea of not having many adults apart from the police about. We therefore were in the 21st century. It gave a form of 'focus'. You may want to include that by suggesting this at the beginning.

Once we had tried and tested the Amnesty workshops it became apparent that they had a wider scope than running through one isolated problem. It seemed that we could also string together a sequence of workshops which would take the theory that bit further. All we needed was new topic matter.

I also wanted to use the experiential nature of what we had done in reverse. Instead of imparting information *to* young people I thought that there must be some way of channelling the information *back* to us. About this time I was also asked to do some work in primary schools on bullying. Having researched the topic thoroughly I worked with three actors teaching them the techniques and then they went into eight schools with workshops written and designed to bring out bullying stories that had actually happened to pupils. The formation of each workshop was similar to what we had done in the Amnesty work. The stories which we got were written and rehearsed in one week into one short anti-bullying play, *Boxing Clever*. The show did three tours, playing to over 20,000 children with over a 95 per cent teachers' approval rating, leading to the play being the most successful I've ever written—why? Because young people used us as a vehicle and the stories that they told rang true to other young people.

Environmental Workshops

Whilst it had been a truly satisfying experience I still felt that the format for workshops needed some work. The format worked—we'd proved that but there needed to be more of a link. Then came the environmental workshops. I wrote them first for the Glasgow City Council's Summer Workshop Programme, rehearsed them again in a youth theatre setting then stuck them out in eight primary schools for four weeks. The stories were again written into a play and rehearsed in one week. It toured for four weeks as *Global Warning*. Both the experiences with the anti-bullying play and the environmental play lead to the three actors involved in each being able to do Theatre In Education with a real knowledge of the issues, thus giving the script a real boost. The script was genuine as it had come directly from the young people. However these workshops were a pinnacle as they now had been worked on in schools, a youth theatre and with a complete bunch of novices off the street.

The environmental workshops follow the same daily format as the Amnesty workshops and are village based. They are five sessions in the extraordinary life of a small village. To help I have dramatically cut the amount to read through. All you need is to know the full problem, the key times, the key information and the possible solutions.

The one significant addition to the Amnesty workshops was the town council. We held ad hoc elections because we needed an accountable body to make decisions on behalf of everybody. You'll see why!

The Format

As with the Amnesty workshops you split the group into six or more 'family' groups—you then create places/houses in the hall which will be used through their sessions. Key times for each day are:

5.00 a.m. Information and sleep
7.00 a.m. Wake up
8.00 a.m. Breakfast
10.40 a.m. Break
Lunch-time
3.00 p.m. Schools out/election
Teatime
Bedime

On day 2 you hold an election for the five council places. Council meets every day. On day 3 of each session you encounter a problem. We, and they, found some comfort in that happening. We therefore had a pattern:

Day 1: Establish/re-establish village.
Day 2: Election.
Day 3: Problem—council get some knowledge.
Day 4/5: Council propose solution after studying detailed report/election.

Workshop One—Global Warming—Water Flooding in Houses

On day 3 at 7 a.m. in the morning one of the households wakes up to find that their kitchen is completely flooded. On day 4 the flooding spreads to other houses. By day 5 the flooding is in every house. If the council do something by day 5 the problem may be solved.

For Council's Eyes Only—(To be given to them at lunch-time—day 3).

The only way to stop the warming up of the environment is to stop using harmful gases. Villagers can ban their very handy cans used for glueing things together. They can walk everywhere instead of using vehicles which produces the gases. Or they can build tall houses on sticks to escape the flooding. As a council you may have to try and make them do these things. This may make you unpopular. You may want to wait and see if things get worse.

For Council's Eyes Only—(To be given to them at lunch-time—day 4).

The ice in the north and south of the world are slowly melting and water in the world is increasing. The number of gases in the world that harm the world have increased by 26 per cent in the last 100 years and will double in the next 100 years. This is because:

- We make electricity by burning coal, oil and gas.
- Transport is another major cause of gases.
- The gases used in things which make our lives more acceptable—glue, cans, aerosols, etc. are a third major cause.

The gases that exist naturally in the Earth's atmosphere let the sun's rays through to warm us, and they also trap some of the sun's heat, rather like the glass in a greenhouse does. If they did not, the Earth would be a frozen planet.

The problem we have to tackle is that the level of gases which trap the sun's heat is rapidly rising and the result is a kind of blanket in the air. The 'blanket' prevents an increasing amount of heat from escaping from the Earth's surface and so the global temperature is beginning to rise.

In the bleak days of a British winter, this may seem to be a good idea. In fact, it could be disastrous.

Council Options Paper

By breakfast on day 5 at the latest the council must decide what to do. You can:

- Ban or restrict the use of harmful gases—but how will you do it or enforce it?
- Stop digging coal and invest in natural energy like wind or sea power but this is extremely expensive.
- Make everyone walk or cycle and stop public transport—but will people like it?
- Invest in cheap atom power that does not use fossil fuels.
- Ignore the problem as experts can get it wrong.

Having dealt with the build up of gases and global warming we turn our attention over to deforestation. Remember that this is a five-session programme and what people have created before they must stick with.

Return family groups to the six or more 'family' groups that were created before with factory, school, homes etc. Run through a day to reaffirm structure. Intervene to give out jobs and ensure that the work is being followed. One person (last week's foreman at the factory) becomes Mr(s) I M Rich. Your council remains as it was elected before.

Workshop Two—Greenbelt—A Factory Application for a Forest

It is Saturday and all the families are going on a day out in the forest. When they return home at teatime each house has had a letter delivered from Mr(s) I M Rich. They want to build a new factory in the forest. There are more than a few people upset at this. On day 4 there will be a public meeting at lunch-time to hear Mr(s) I M Rich's plans. On day 5 the council will take the decision over the planning application before the council elections which are postponed from day 2. The council has to be careful because the forest on the edge of the village is used by everyone for picnics and for leisure. Mr(s) I M Rich has applied for permission to build a paper factory in the forest. The village needs jobs and this will provide plenty.

For Council Eyes Only—(To be given at lunch-time on day 3).

Trees give off oxygen and absorb carbon dioxide therefore fewer trees mean less oxygen. Humans give off carbon dioxide and breathe in oxygen. Many animals and birds live in trees and hedgerows. Nearly 100 different species each day die. If the forest is cut down the very rare blue-spotted dodobilled platydog will die off.

For Council Eyes Only—(To be given at lunch-time on day 4).

The only way to save the forest is to stop the planning permission.

Council Options Paper
The council can:

- Reject the planning application.
- Swap building the factory in the forest for building it in one of the villages.
- Make everyone recycle paper so that trees won't need to be cut down.
- Invest in the factory and make Mr(s) I M Rich sign a contract promising certain things for the villagers.

You have another new council elected straight after the factory decision who have dealt with the harmful gases and planning applications. You want now to turn to scarce natural resources.

Split groups back into their six or more 'family' groups—recreate factory, school, homes etc. Run through two days to reaffirm structure.

Problem is:

Workshop Three—Lights Off—Natural Resources

On the third day all the lights and all of the electricity in the village goes out. There is no heat, light or anything. The school has to shut as does the factory and apart from having nowhere to cook food there is only a few days supply left.

For Council Eyes Only—(To be given at breakfast time on day 3).

All the dead dinosaurs which have been dug up for many years to provide fuel are running out. They are burnt to provide electricity but there are alternative ways of creating electricity. You could try wind power with lots of big windmills which is expensive or water power but you'd have to build big dams. Atomic power would provide electricity quickly and cheaply. You may have a half days grace before a decision **must** be made.

For Council Eyes Only—(To be given at lunch-time on day 4).

Fossil fuels: Coal, oil and gas are all fossil fuels. Like most of the energy on Earth, they were produced by the heat of the sun. Coal is the fossilised remains of small plants and dinosaurs that lived on the Earth millions of years ago. But unlike other forms of natural energy, fossil fuels will not last forever. Their supply is limited; once we have used them all up, we cannot replace them. The 'environmentalists' term for this kind of energy is 'non-renewable'. Burning fossil fuels releases sulphur dioxide, nitrogen oxides, carbon dioxide, soot, ash and dust into the atmosphere. These pollutants contribute to the greenhouse effect and cause acid rain.

Energy: We must save energy.

Alternative energy sources: Within the next 100 years or so, we will have to find energy from alternative sources. This is because fossil fuels will all have been used up, apart from coal. Of course, we also need alternative sources so that we can put a stop to pollution. Unless there is some amazing new discovery, these alternative sources of energy will be the renewable resources described below.

Renewable resources can provide different sources of energy, such as heat, movement and electricity. They can be produced near to the areas where they are needed, so that no energy is wasted in transporting or transmitting them. Most of them produce little or no pollution, and they will never run out.

Let's take a detailed look at these resources and their advantages and disadvantages.

Solar power: The sun is the ultimate source of all energy on Earth. Even in our cloudy country, it could provide 100 times more energy than we need if we could harness it. It's silent, clean and renewable. At the moment it's only used in a very small way for heating buildings and water. An even smaller capacity is used for generating electricity.

Water power: The simplest form of water power is the water-mill. These have been known in Britain since Roman times. A water-mill works by the damming of a stream above the mill. The water then cascades down on to the paddles of the wheel and forces it to turn. The wheel drives machinery inside the mill, to grind corn, for example. Water-mills are still used in many parts of the world.

Hydroelectricity: Is a more sophisticated kind of water power. It's clean, efficient and produces 6.7 per cent of the world's energy. Modern water-wheels, called water turbines, are a ring of curved blades. They are turned by fast-flowing water so that they drive generators. Hydroelectricity produces energy that is cheap and constantly available. It has several disadvantages though. One is that building the stations is expensive. Another is that dams are usually needed and so much land is flooded. This means that the local ecology is damaged and people often have to leave their homes. A third disadvantage is that silt can build up to make the station unusable. Careful planning can lessen the damage to the environment—for example, fish ladders make it possible for fish to move upstream and down.

Wave power: The power in the movement of waves has interested scientists since the 18th century. In the last 20 years, Britain and Norway have tried to turn this movement into electricity.

Scientists think that for every metre a wave rises or falls in mid-ocean, 100 kilowatts of electricity could be generated. Nearer to the shore, it would be about 15 kilowatts—enough to power five large electric fires.

Wind power: Winds are created by the air being unevenly heated by the sun. Warm air rises, cool air flows in to take its place, and a wind is created. Windmills have been used for over 1,000 years and you can still see them in many parts of the world. The wind drives the sails, which drive machinery inside the mill.

Modern windmills are called wind turbines. Wind speeds increase above the ground, so the blades are placed high up on poles, or towers. Inside the towers are generators. Some wind turbines have blades as long as 196 feet (60 metres). The blades can be turned to face the wind or turned away if the wind is too strong for them. Some of these modern wind turbines are controlled by computers.

Geothermal power: The surface of the Earth is cool, but its centre is made of hot, molten rock. When a volcano erupts it hurls this rock, which we call lava, out into the air. In some parts of the world, the Earth's surface has cracks in the rock that allow water to rise as steam until it reaches the surface, where the temperature turns it back into hot water. Sometimes the pressure forces the water high into the air, and this is known as a geyser.

All the alternatives cost more money.

Council Options Paper
You could:

- Build lots of windmills—but where?
- Build lots of dams which may be expensive.
- Build an Atomic Power Station which is very cheap.
- Ignore the problems as this has happened before—ages ago—and nothing happened then.
- Invest in solar power which may take time to put together.

An election is held on the morning of day 5.

You move onto acid rain with yet another council. By now a pattern may be emerging as to who the young people trust (or don't) to be their elected representatives. It is interesting at this point to chart political careers. If you find that you're **not** getting the numbers to stand for the council you can ban elections until the end of the workshops.

Split the group back into their six or more 'family' groups—recreate factory, school, homes etc. Run through two days. Remember that any decisions in weeks 1–4 will have an effect. Intervene when necessary to give out jobs and ensure that work is being followed.

Workshop Four—Statue Eroding—Acid Rain

One of the children in the school has noticed that all the flowers in their garden are starting to die. Then their best friend falls very ill. Everyone is very worried about them. The war monument is also starting to crumble and just last week a large part of it fell down and nearly hit someone.

For Council Eyes Only—(To be given at lunch-time on day 3).

The local newspaper has reported that a factory has been putting out pollution for years. This factory has been dumping chemicals in the rivers as well as putting harmful gases into the atmosphere. The pollution destroys stone, plant life and causes disease in people. The factory is in a town 300 miles away.

For Council Eyes Only—(To be given at breakfast time on day 4).

Acid rain: Acid rain has caused much damage in Europe and the United States. In the States, forests in Vermont are dying because of the pollution from a power station in Ohio, 1,000 miles (1,610 kilmotres) away. The trees in Europe are dying too—64% of them in Britain and 50 per dent in Germany, Czechoslovakia, Greece, Sweden, Belgium and Holland are also badly affected.

In southern Norway, nearly all the lakes and streams are dead, that is, no animals or plants can live in them because they are too acid. The acid rain has dissolved metals and other pollutants and washed them into the water. It washes metal into drinking water too, and this can cause serious illness. In Sweden, people's hair has even turned green because of the amount of copper in their water supply.

In Greece, the Parthenon is crumbling. It has stood for over 2,000 years, but it cannot withstand the corrosive action of acid rain. Nor can the Taj Mahal in India nor St Paul's Cathedral in London. Many buildings, and even railway lines, are being destroyed by acid rain.

Fortunately, there is good news. Something is being done to halt the damage, although progress is slow.

A law was passed in the United States in 1981 that all cars must be fitted with catalytic converters. These filter out a lot of the nitrogen oxides, as well as carbon monoxide and hydrocarbons, and can reduce the pollution from cars by up to 70 per cent. They can only be fitted to cars that run on unleaded petrol. The European Community agreed in 1992 that catalytic converters must be fitted to all new small cars.

President Bush announced in June 1989 that the US production of acid rain would be reduced by more than half in the next ten years. As from 1995, cars built in the US run on non-petrol fuels such as ethanol and gasohol.

The first flue gas desulphurisation system in Britain was fitted at the Drax Power Station in 1994; this reduces emissions of sulphur dioxide. There are plans to build natural gas-fired power stations at a number of sites in northern England and Wales. These will give off less carbon dioxide and nitrogen oxide and no sulphur dioxide at all.

Environmental groups say that a lot more needs to be done before the Earth will benefit from these measures. But at least we have made a start in the right direction.

In 1886, black snow fell in Scotland. It is the result of particles of dirt in the air. Six years later, in 1872, the term 'acid rain' was coined. And that's a good example of how long it has taken us to wake up to what we are doing to the environment.

We now use 'acid rain' to describe all kinds of pollutants that are carried up into the air and fall back to Earth in the form of rain, snow or fog. The pollutants combine with the moisture in other chemicals. The rain formed like this is between 4 and a 1,000 times more acid than normal rainfall. When it falls to Earth it damages trees, lakes and streams, buildings and people.

The main chemical culprits that reach the atmosphere are sulphur dioxide and nitrogen oxides. Natural events such as forest fires and volcanic eruptions are responsible for a certain amount, but these chemicals are produced in much larger quantities by the burning of fossil fuels—gas, coal and oil.

Power stations produce much of the sulphur dioxide. They can be fitted with devices called flue gas desulphurisation systems to cut the amount of gas given off, but in Britain we have not yet done this. Power stations produce nitrogen oxides too, as do other industrial processes, and half of them come from vehicle exhausts.

Council Options Paper
You could:

- Ask for the factory to be closed and lay off all the workers.
- Ask for the factory to stop and help to invest in another factory that is more environmentally conscious.
- Tell the factory that it must adhere to new environment laws which you will pass.
- Defend the right of the factory to keep making its product and keep people in jobs.

On day 5 there is an election. The girl's fate is in the hands of the group!

Workshop Five—Rubbish in the Streets—Recycling

This is the last workshop and there is a surprise at the end of it. You should prepare a list of everyone in the village as a ballot paper. At the end of the workshop there shall be an election but not for the council.

Return all groups to their six or more 'family' groups—recreate factory, school, homes etc. Run through two days to reaffirm your structure.

On day 2 the binmen took away the rubbish as normal except they didn't give out black rubbish bags as they usually do. On day 3 the rubbish still needs to be put out except there are no rubbish bags and there will be a smelly build up as the day goes on.

For Council Eyes Only—(To be given at lunch-time on day 3).

The factory that makes plastic bags has closed down due to the amount of pollution it was causing. It does have some plastic bags left. The tin factory is also about to close down because of the pollution. It makes aluminium cans for drinks and food. They also have a lot of cans stockpiled. Both factories are not going to be used after they close.

For Council Eyes Only—(To be given at lunch-time on day 4).

Before you throw anything away, stop and think. Might someone else have a use for it?

Charities are often pleased to have old stamps, silver paper, toys, books, magazines and old clothes. Reuse the paper, polythene bags and plastic carrier bags. When you go shopping, take a carrier bag with you. When the bags are too tatty to hold the shopping, use them for putting rubbish in so that it stays neatly in the dustbin instead of spilling out to create litter.

Farm shops and wholefood shops are often pleased to have egg boxes back. Don't throw used envelopes away—send them off a second time with a sticker explaining that this is to save trees. You can buy these stickers in most wholefood shops—and, of course, they are made from recycled paper!

If you have a garden but no compost heap, start one. It's an excellent way of recycling potato peelings, apple cores, tea leaves—all the vegetable rubbish that comes from the kitchen. A good compost heap is also the first step towards successful gardening without chemicals because you can use it to fertilise the soil.

Take as much rubbish as you can to local recycling centres. There's a bottle bank in most towns these days. Save up all your jars and bottles and take them to it. Take off the tops first and don't leave the bag or box you took them in as litter!

You can probably find someone who will take your newspapers for recycling. Try the local council first. If they don't take them, ask around—there may be a local conservation group which will be glad to help. If you are stuck, ask Friends of the Earth.

Some councils also recycle plastic and aluminium and some will actually pay you for the aluminium cans. You can expect to get around 30p for 50 cans. This doesn't sound a lot but we use over 2,000 million aluminium cans each year. This works out to about £20,000,000 for the people who are smart enough to return them!

There are over 250 centres to take your cans to. They will give you reusable bags to collect them in and a magnetic tester so you can be sure which ones are aluminium.

If you have a choice, avoid buying packaged goods. If the goods you want are on the counter both packaged and unpackaged, choose the unpackaged ones. You may find that the storekeeper will try to wrap them just as much, but say that you don't want the extra wrapping and explain politely why not. If you think that something has got far too much packaging, you can complain to the Packaging Council.

Don't waste paper. Don't use the throwaway paper products such as tissues, kitchen paper and napkins—ask your parents to buy cotton ones instead. When you are writing, use both sides of the paper. If you have any paper that has already been used on one side, it will do for rough paper.

Buy recycled paper products. Toilet paper made from recycled paper is on sale in many supermarkets, so persuade your parents that it's a good idea to buy it. You can probably find attractive stationery, exercise books and greetings cards too.

Council Options Paper

You could:

- Turn the factories into recycling centres.
- Close both factories, build a new one under the new environmental laws and employ all the workers again.
- Ban plastics and cans and invest in new types of packaging for holding food and rubbish—like paper.
- Give the factories money if they can restart working and change all the laws to allow them to keep producing plastic and tin.
- It's all the villagers' fault anyway for using up so much, so ignore it.

Final Solution?

On day 5 you call everyone together at teatime. The decisions in each week has led to five decisions now having been made. Due to the mess that has been made of the planet a spaceship will take off at breakfast on day 6 to find a new planet to live on. Dependent upon the decisions made in each week up to two seats on the spaceship are available, up to a maximum of ten. The environmentally good villagers get ten seats. On day 5 the village will record their votes as to who will go on the ship. The most popular (?) or the most able (?) get to go.

The twist, of course, is that we can't get off this planet and it is therefore more important that we apply the lessons learned over the last five weeks.

The obvious next step was for the young people to perform to other young people. With these environmental workshops in eight Ayrshire schools we were provided with eight excellent stories with solutions for each problem. The format of improvising as a whole group had lead to a form of security which allowed them to create within a structure which was tightly organised but from outside did **not** look organised. I had thought that using their material was a reward of some sorts but the ultimate prize had to be them performing themselves. Unfortunately I was unable to achieve that with this material, but having tackled bullying, the environment and human rights I went a bit soft and tackled Scottish History.

ACT TWO, SCENE I
AN INTRODUCTION TO PERFORMANCE

Now that we've dealt with the workshops and developed into what is a crossover between the workshop process and the performances, I'm going to concentrate on performance. I have included some improvised 'starters', however the second Act assumes that you have a play you wish to perform.

It is worth noting that the beauty of improvised performances as opposed to script work is that much of the resources you will need will be your choice rather than that of an author who has a penchent for 17th-century carriage clocks etc! In that case you may want to cross off as much as you can in the project plan and work out roughly how long it might take to rehearse ready for the stage. A very rough guide is usually one and a half minutes per page of script and eight hours of rehearsal per five minutes of performance. Hefty? You bet! But first a little introduction that concentrates on what you should perform.

In 1994, I started running the local youth theatre on my own. After five years of being part of a theatre company, with revenue funding by the Scottish Arts Council and which had a 21-year track record, it was a scary prospect to find that I no longer had allegedly immense resources behind me. Over the next few years I was to be involved in some very important decisions on the future of that youth theatre. In Scotland for some 15 years community education had been the preserve of the regional council, and leisure that of the district council. Youth work was a regional function, youth theatre a district function. When local authority reorganisation happened so too did a clash of culture. For some leisure departments that had been foreseen and youth theatre had become more youth empowered. In our largely middle class town the youth theatre was expected to do the 'standards' and draw large crowds. Their latest performance piece had not sold well and there was a lack of conviction amongst the members of the youth theatre itself that it was following the right 'direction' for them. The play, *Zigger Zagger* by Peter Terson had been a leap too far. We felt we had to consider:

- The 'type' of play needed to meet both ours and our funders' needs.
- The venues and types of venue we wished to perform in.
- A realistic reason for choosing the texts we wanted to perform.

These were important becausc:

- We needed to re-establish the group and draw in the crowds. We therefore decided to pick a popular play that was widely recognisable.
- The last production had played in a 615-seat theatre to 100/200 people. It was almost soul destroying. We needed to look sold out and so we went to a smaller space.
- The reason for choosing a recognisable play was not only to re-establish the youth group but also to give the members back faith in what they were doing.

It was in the desire to 'push back the boundaries' of this youth theatre that it was forgotten that there were young people who actually wanted to perform popular musicals. By preventing them from doing so, their aspirations were squashed rather than liberated. The youth theatre had already done similar musicals but had never done *Bugsy Malone*. It packed them in over two nights at a smaller venue and was proudly performed.

It was a triumph but left us again with a few challenges. From a member shop of 40 we now had 80 kids from 9-years to 16-years of age wanting to perform the next play. We had to consider the youth group's size to be a factor in what to do next. It was felt that the group was too big so we split them into two age ranges.

We now applied the logic of three previous questions but now not to one youth theatre production but to two; the younger group show and the older group show. The split it has to be said was done arbitrarily. We had enough capable primary school age kids for the younger group.

The key questions now became:

1. What was the youth theatre's ability?
2. What were the venues we wished to perform in and the audience we needed to reach?
3. What was the reason for the texts that we chose?
4. What 'type' of play should we therefore perform.

The Younger Group

We had chosen to cut the youth theatre where we had because an 8 or 9-year old would not be able to hold together a two hour show, however we had some pretty able 11 to 12-year olds. I knew of an absolutely cracking play called *The Incredible Vanishing* by Denise Coffey which was *not* condescending and exceptionally good for younger kids. It was not a well-known play but the youth theatre had gone a long way with *Bugsy* to re-establish itself and we did not need to work hard to bring in the droves of people. We wanted to extend the experience of our younger ones. It was vital that they got real quality work to do. *The Incredible Vanishing* fitted the bill. We stayed at the smaller venue to keep the success and build our audience. However, we made a conscious decision against doing socially challenging work which had temporarily lost some of the core audience, or work written specifically for the youth theatre. It was therefore chosen specifically to keep our profile up and the work ongoing.

There was an element of 'safety' involved. The audience came in droves, the young actors were superb and the audience were asking about what we would be doing next.

The Older Group

When considering what to do with them I knew they were very good, could hold together two hours without any problems but we needed to consider very carefully what venue they would perform in. Why? The cute factor. When you're 10 your auntie thinks you're cute and you love to perform for her. When you're 15 and full of spots you don't want your auntie to embarrass you. Audiences are also very reticent about coming to watch 'amateur' 15-year olds pretending to be 40-year old fathers in a 'socially challenging performance piece'. It takes time to educate and develop an audience professionally with your style and convince them that you know what you're doing! We opted for going out on tour to primary schools. The venues therefore had a ready-made audience for the work. It allowed our older kids to work on challenging acting *and* play to over 200 people at almost every venue. That left the 'type' of play. As we were going out to primary schools it was important that the text was understandable and accessible. We therefore went on a ten venue tour of *Telling Wilde Tales*, an adaptation of seven of Oscar Wilde's *Fairy Tales* by Jules Tasca. It managed to fulfil all of our wishes *but* due to the timing of both these productions, we had done the younger group in June and the older one in September, the size of the youth theatre had dropped. Not a disaster.

We were beginning to be noticed. One word we hadn't used in our work was 'original'. We had quite deliberately worked through 'classics' to other work to reassure our audience that what you got when you saw us was enjoyable theatre. Now we had an audience it was time to challenge them. With a smaller number of 'seasoned' actors we could. Our originality however came not from writing something for the youth theatre but from performing the World Theatre Premiere of Mel Brooks and Gene Wilder's *Young Frankenstein*. We returned to the larger venue triumphant and with something we were very proud to present. It took three years—that's three years to rebuild. Three whole years. Your first show might sell out but if you want to keep things going, plan shows 2 and 3 whilst doing show 1.

What we had done in all instances was to analyse why we wanted to perform, what we needed to perform and then find something to fit the bill. There are therefore a variety of options in performing and can be simply split into the following categories:

1. Already written (See Epilogue)
   —Standard musicals: *Grease*, *Return to the Forbidden Planet* etc.
   —Standard texts: Shakespeare, Pinter etc.
   —Young persons' plays: *Whale*, *Zigger Zagger* etc.
2. Not already written
   —Commissioned work: written specifically for the youth theatre.
   —Improvised work: written by young people perhaps with an outside writer or by themselves.

N.B. Remember that this is very crude split. You can take a standard text or well-known story and cut to suit yourself. If a standard text then get permission first.

What I've attended to in my first examples were all pre-written works in some shape. However I was not always just employed to run a local authority youth theatre with a history of standard performances. With the right social work group and youth group with a special interest I got involved in different types of performances which were written specifially for these types of groups.

However we applied the same questions to their types of performances.

- What 'type' of play or performance was needed?
- In which venue would we wish to perform?
- What were our reasons for performing?

Sometimes however, I wasn't too successful. I once decided to take a youth theatre out on a tour for Christmas. We had been performing and working in the local community centre for years but found that we had out-grown it. We moved our base to the local academy and now our members were sufficiently able, and the group of the right size to be split into two rather than just to perform one show at Christmas. We were an established group and we carefully planned a small four venue tour performing in the evening. Two of these venues were in schools and performed to a grand total of 23 people! Our greatest audience was at the over 65 club when ten attended thinking there was bingo on! It taught me a salutary lesson.

Picking the right venue can also help to solve one of your biggest potential problems. To sell tickets for a youth show, in fact to drum up an audience to any show is one of, if not *the*, most difficult things to do. The second play for any new youth group for example is often more difficult to sell tickets for than the novelty ridden first play. By play three it has become more and more difficult.

A 'tour' to various venues is something well worth contemplating, however remember to take a performance which does not include the technical mastery that transforms stages into Cinderella's kitchens or back alleyways full of dancing felines. (It can also be expensive but if your venues are schools, clubs etc. and hence with ready-made audiences you can avoid some of the pitfalls.)

Drama has a magic all of its own which connects with children without having to dress up the principal characters in tights. Spending time rehearsing something worthwhile is much better time spent than raking through costume racks for the right colour of the principal boy's tights. If you can't remember your scene—looking good won't make you look better.

A small visit to old folk's homes or to the local youth clubs cements communal ties as well as being a good marketing tool should you ever wish to increase your selling base.

And what 'type' of play is needed! Wee Brian doing impressions and Susan singing *Wild Rover* out of tune with her sister on banjo won't pack them in. Similarly a socially challenging drugs piece won't find many nursery schools booking! You have to compromise sometimes between your message and your audience. It can be done without compromising your principles at all. All you have to do is consider whether your performance piece matches your audience

It is worth looking around and catalogues from French's or Warner Chappell give you a good survey of what 'standards' are on offer.

For the slightly more adventurous you may want to hit on the many youth theatre websites including www.drama.org.uk. They have play lists of less well-known material.

Before we consider these however, a word about organisation. To do **any** performance from a one-man show to an epic needs organisation. We have that cunning plan! Here is the explanation of it!

ACT TWO, SCENE 2
PERFORMANCE GUIDE

This is not the absolute idiot's guide but something which will hopefully help you through the anxious bits.

Jobs—A Diagram to Help

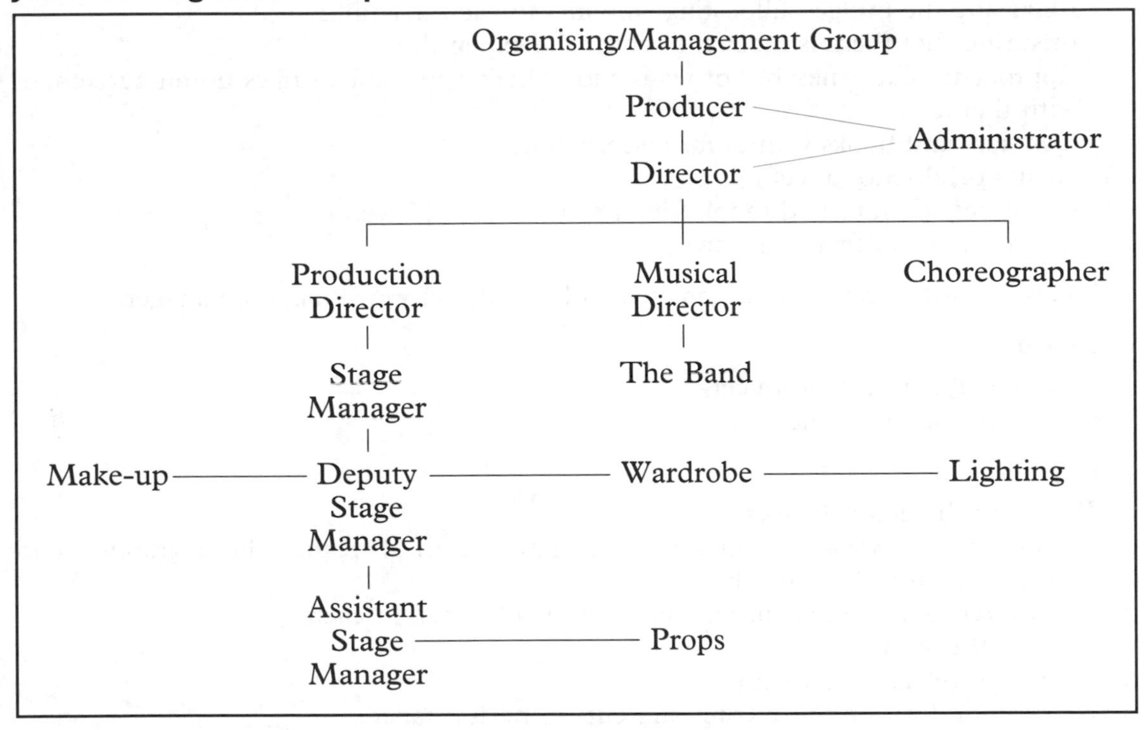

Each of the job descriptions which follow are pretty basic. I have not touched upon costume design, lighting design, marketing, publicity, front of house staff, sound specialists, fight directors, stage designers or the plethora of other specialists who inhabit the theatre. It is easy to believe that they are somewhat 'invented' as there are so many and they can be so 'specialised', however believe me they are highly skilled jobs which, when they can be afforded in a production, add immense amounts to it. If you really want to know how much actors depend on these people, count at the end of your favourite TV show in the credits, the number of backstage people against the number of actors involved.

But what do they do and when should they do it? The guide can be used with improvised pieces if the writing has been done or you are confident that it will be ready in three months. Perhaps the most important tip is to remember that sticking a seven foot high silver reindeer in at the dress rehearsal may artistically add to your production but might not be possible for the stage manager to find, so like every boy scout—**be prepared**!

Producer

- Responsible to organising committee or just yourself.
- Responsible for everyone!

Main duties:

1. Organising the production team.
2. Supervising their roles.
3. Negotiating the financial affairs of the production.
4. Finalising the budget, allocating amounts to each heading.
5. Ensuring that there is income to cover the expenditure.
6. Approaches each member of team and, where applicable, draws up an agreement with them.
7. Contacts and books venues for performances.
8. Chairs production meetings.
9. Initial negotiations and monitoring negotiations with venues.
10. Approves list of first night invites.

The main duties can be amalgamated with the director/production manager.

Director

- Responsible to the producer.
- Responsible for the actors.

Main tasks

1. Directing the actors onstage.
2. Negotiating between production manager, technical team, choreographer and musical director of the production.
3. Taking rehearsals, their format and what will happen in each.
4. Casting the show.
5. Draws up rehearsal schedule.
6. Make final decision on rewrites and cuts in performance.

The main duties can be amalgamated with the producer/choreographer/musical director.

Administrator

- Responsible to director/producer.
- Responsible for no one.

Main tasks

1. Book rehearsal room.
2. Communicate rehearsal times, dates and venues with cast.
3. Arrange tickets.
4. Arrange publicity.

5. Fills booking forms in for rehearsals and performances.
6. Arranges licences for performances.
7. Set up and hold administration folder.
8. First night invites.
9. The programme.
10. Ticket sales.

The main duties can be amalgamated with the producer.

Musical Director

- Responsible to director/producer.
- Responsible for band (if one is used).

Main tasks

1. Taking band rehearsals.
2. Taking singing rehearsals.
3. The arrangements to be used.
4. Playing at the performances.
5. Make decisions on cuts and rewrites on music in plays.

The main duties can be amalgamated with the director.

Choreographer

- Responsible to director/producer.
- Responsible for no one.

Main tasks

1. Interpret the music and teach their dance to the company.
2. Take dance rehearsals.
3. Make cuts and re-choreograph dances in play.

The main duties can be amalgamated with the director.

Production Manager

- Responsible to director/producer.
- Responsible for stage management crew.

Main tasks

1. Advising director on technical details and taking responsibility for them.
2. Building the set.
3. Ensuring the costumes are hired
4. Ensuring adequate lighting.
5. Ensuring adequate sound.
6. Monitoring the budget for the production.
7. Establishes dates of production plan and holds it.
8. Make detailed negotiations with venues.
9. Make venue visits and recommend any changes necessary.

The main duties can be amalgamated with the producer.

Stage Manager

- Responsible to production manager/director.
- Responsible for deputy and assistant stage manager.

Main tasks

1. To run the show from the book.
2. To check the props are there on each night.
3. To return borrowed equipment.
4. Day to day contact with venues.
5. Building the set.

The main duties can be amalgamated with the production manager.

Deputy Stage Manager

- Responsible to stage manager.
- Responsible for no one.

Main tasks

1. Finding the props.
2. Working lights and sound.
3. Plotting lighting.
4. Building the set.
5. Running the technical side of the show.

The main duties can be amalgamated with the stage manager.

Assistant Stage Manager

- Responsible to stage manager.
- Responsible for no one.

Main tasks

1. The book.
2. Helping to run the show.
3. Organising and supervising costumes.

The main duties can be amalgamated with the deputy stage manager/stage manager.

Peformance Handbook

The most important aspect of the sheets which follow is that they serve as a form of 'reminder' that certain things **ought** to be done. For example, you will know that there are props to be got for a production but the production may not be ready for them until week 12. However, you will not forget about props if you leave spaces blank when they are mentioned in the sheets and each week remind yourself that it is to be done.

There are other issues which may require you to change direction mid-way in a particular project which can upset the plans that you have made. When these things happen it is important that you ensure the administrivia is covered allowing the creativity to flow. It is also important to use these sheets as points of contact between yourself and other members of your team. The producer will have responsibility to see that things are **done** in the weeks that are detailed but not necessarily to do them themselves. It is important that more than one person understands why there are very good reasons as to why some things can't be done. This is a very tight 15-week turn around. Realistically you might want to double it—or just live dangerously!

Production Instructions

Week 1

1. Play agreed

2. Everyone knows what they are doing

3. Budget finalised

A final figure is agreed for props, set, costume, technical and transport. Figures are then passed to assistant producer/production manager so that they can keep an eye on the budget.

4. Personnel appointed

All specialists are contacted and contracts drawn up.

5. Venues finalised for performance

A decision is taken on which venues to approach and what basis is the performance going to be on, i.e. for charity/profit share etc. Venues then contacted to book in final rehearsal dates and performance dates. Remember that you will want to rehearse in the performance venue (unless on tour) before you open the show.

6. Research begun

If required all members of cast/production team undertake research on the topic to inform writer/actors/director/producer as to possible creative avenues.

7. Project plan completed

You're reading it!

8. Administrative folder set up

Should include:

- Database forms: Particularly names, addresses, emergency contact numbers etc.
- Registers: Each rehearsal has tick/signing in sheets so we know who's 'in'.
- Schedules: Spare ones for parents whose little darlings forget.
- Relevant correspondence: The licence, letters given out etc.

9. First rehearsal finalised

Calling together of whole cast set up for forthcoming week 3. It is important that this is planned as you want to start professionally.

Week 2

1. Arrange rehearsals—book venues

Make sure somewhere is booked for all the cast to rehearse in. Consider what you will do for the *first* rehearsal.

2. Rehearsal schedule drawn up

Draw up weeks 2–6 for cast members. You will find more about how to draw one up later

Week 3

1. Production meeting 1

All technical staff are requested to participate in enunciating their demands. Take each thought which is not your own seriously!

2. Rehearsal schedules weeks 2–6 issued

Schedules drawn up are checked before being given out to cast.

3. Posters and leaflets decision

Should you have a budget, take a decision on what publicity is to be distributed. Such publicity should form a separate timetable. Create that timetable now in consultation with your production staff.

4. Cast the show and measure them

Decide fairly early on who plays who and cast accordingly. You will also want to measure them for costumes. Start now to organise costumes. Use the character sheets for each cast member.

Week 4

1. Rewrites discussed

Writer(s) of the improvisation performances will receive a wide cross-section of views regarding their product after first rehearsals and should be sent off with ideas and a strict timescale. Again another timetable may need to be established. For established texts you may want to cut scenes or cut out sections. Timetable decisions to be made now as actors need some time to get used to changes of 'cuts'! Check your licence to see if you need to have text cuts approved.

2. Venues contacted again re timetable

Venues are contacted again to check on tour dates, get in/get out times making sure that janitors/caretakers know what's going on.

3. Check on venues for performances

After your first production meeting you will have some idea of what technical equipment and challenges you will now have. Make arrangements for a physical tour of where the production is going. Note down any peculiarly distinctive features worthy of note. Organise now any extra lighting, sound equipment etc.

4. Music discussed

If you are using any music make sure you have permission and/or someone to play/organise it.

5. Venues contacted re requirements

Venues should be followed up with letters, re whose coming/when they're coming as confirmation of your phone call.

Week 5

1. 'The book' ready

The stage manager's bible. There is more on the book and how to make it up later. It should be ready to be 'used' in rehearsals. The book is the rehearsal plan which the ASM will give to the stage manager so that they can run the show—(pencils, rubbers, patience and paper essential).

2. Props list
Based on script, scene by scene list of props. Source and price—do not buy yet because things may get 'cut'.

3. Production meeting 2
Agenda :
—Cost of props
—Cuts (probable)
—Budget
—The set—deadline week 8—who's designing it?
—Stage management team—who is definitely doing what?

4. Open Booking
Start selling tickets early. We organise a booking night in advance of the show.

Week 6
1. Posters and leaflets deadline
Should there have been a 'yes' to publicity, the dates, times, prices, logo, details for posters set up and ready to be proofread. Again a separate timetable for distribution may be being followed for publicity. You will want to establish poster points and who will ask the kindly shopkeeper to put it in their windows! Cast are useful for this I find!

2. History/biogs for programme
All members of the youth theatre to be featured are asked to provide material for the programme. Now you may want to talk your friendly parent with the PC into printing off flyers.

3. Technical requirements list
A list of lighting/sound/the flash equipment which may need to be hired, given to producer for approval. Checked against ideas for set. Alert stage management team.

4. Budget checked
Technical requirements/props lists checked off against budget.

Week 7
1. Set list for stage managers
Although your stage manager *will* be involved in most discussions you will have to tell them things need to be built or bought or sourced or borrowed. All items are then sought for, smallest amount of money possible.

2. Props list version 2
New props list. Review of version 1 to provide, hopefully, the definitive list. Check off against director's wishes and 'the book'.

Week 8
1. Deadline for set design
Last opportunity for the two or three dimensional plan to be in place which shall be the basis of production. Cost out things needing to be bought and order them for week 9, i.e. wood. Use stage management team as much as possible.

2. Rehearsal props bought and introduced
The definitive list of props is bought for the purposes of rehearsal. Allow no one to take them home with them and box them after each rehearsal in a **clearly** marked skull and cross bones container.

3. Production meeting 3
Should it be required (I usually find that it is), set up yet another meeting for everyone to air opinions. Publicity may be a priority for discussion, including programme copy apart from the biographies. Also settle the issue of where, audience is coming from. By now you'll know initial ticket sales level. Do extra tickets need to be ordered/distributed/ sold? Whilst we may want to spend 4 to 5 hours discussing the types of gels to be used in lights 20 minutes on attracting an audience may be more fruitful.

Week 9

1. Set building
With the design in one hand and the saw in the other, galvanise your stage management team into building. You have two weeks in which to organise the set. Leave the ASM to attend rehearsals on behalf of DSM/stage manager/production manager.

2. Poster/leaflet distribution
Posters and leaflets should be in and a list of distribution already established. In this week the publicity should go out.

3. Run off invite list
Ask everyone to suggest names/addresses for the producer to look through for first night invites.

Week 10

1. Building of set continues
Check on the progress and chat with the producer should there be any problems. Never be optimistic.

2. Press release
To be written up and checked with producer and director. A good photo opportunity to accompany it would be helpful.

3. Programme copy
All the copy to be typed so that the following week it can be checked.

4. Invites out
Ensure producer has gone through the list scoring out any that don't need an invite and send out to the final list.

5. Check props list
Ensure that original props do not need repair or replacement and find out if the props that are now needed are definitely to be used before buying.

6. Production meeting
Final hitches and problems—there will be many!

7. Look again at bookings
Check tickets on sale at box office and how well they are doing. Should you require any additional selling points—organise now!

Week 11

1. Build and paint set

Set **ought** to be completed and simply need to be painted. However, be pessimistic still.

2. Design lighting

Make out, if necessary, a separate lighting plot from 'the book'.

3. Organise stage crew

Make sure they know call times and schedules as well as their responsibilities during the show. You may have to rehearse them separately so they know exactly what they are doing.

4. Letters to parents

It's easy to forget them. However, whoever is caring for your cast at home whilst you're not, will have several questions to ask about the last two weeks of intense rehearsals. I try and save the first 20 minutes of rehearsals by answering as many of these questions as possible. Please alter the letter to suit yourself but be aware that you will be asked these, and other questions.

Week 12

1. Run lighting

Spend time checking lighting rig and plot with stage manger and DSM.

2. Run stage crew

Get them all together and do a show without the cast.

3. Press release/photo-call

Dependent upon bookings, organise final press push.

4. Technical rehearsal

Whole crew, cast, production staff rehearsal.

5. Production meeting

After the technical rehearsal. The agenda will set itself.

6. Allocate dressing rooms

Ensure that a democratic framework is adopted to allow pals 'n' stars to be intertwined and not all crammed in the N dressing room. Also take care that no males mix (adult or otherwise) unsupervised with females.

Week 13

1. Planning of returns

All items borrowed must be planned for returning at the end of the show's run. This is vital as finishing the job ought to be a strong point.

2. Show report

Any technical/artistic/other problems and/or event which is significant is written up in the folder, dated and signed as a record. Also, whether the show went well or not.

Week 14

1. Returns

All returns are away. Don't tick anything off until it has finally gone.

2. Post-mortem
Show reports set the agenda. External audit of project as you want feedback from audience members known to cast. Whole cast attends.

3. Final record keeping
In advance of an internal assessment you need to know final income and expenditure, numbers involved **and** audience figures.

Week 15

1. Assessment
Internal audit of project. Production team meet to discuss.

Extras to Consider

Dress rehearsal
Empty theatre, run show as if an audience are in. Vital. Tradition states that a bad dress rehearsal makes a good first night—as if . . .

Notes to cast
director gives productive and positive criticism. Don't spare blushes if someone is out of line but remember that your cast are volunteers and **can** walk out even at this stage!

Audience figures
Record in show report. Vital as evidence of your worth.

ACT TWO, SCENE 3
THE DIRECTOR'S NOTES

Should you be preparing for the school assembly, parent's night, Glasgow Royal Concert Hall or whatever, performances can be very harrowing for young people. The most important aspect of what you do is that it looks good and does the amount of work you have put into it credit. Here's a few simple tips to help the director and actor alike. As the director—go on, share them!

Keep it Simple

Nobody will expect a Lloyd Webber in the school hall. Pick a simple song, simple actions, a wee piece of drama and then make it look good. **Your** confidence must build before the young people can place confidence in **you**. Too many *Joseph and His Amazing Technicolor Dreamcoat*'s have been performed with massive casts who have acted badly when the choir singing all the songs was really all the head-teacher wanted.

Stop Pretending

I don't mean that the audiences will accept any old rubbish but that if you look like you're driving a horse drawn-carriage they'll believe that you are. An audience will accept what they are given if you believe it. No one believes that the man playing Hamlet is a Danish Prince who's racked with grave and serious doubts over sticking a sword in someone who killed their dad. We know we are in a theatre and that the man will **not** actually kill someone else but just pretend to. Yet I have seen fathers fight over doorbell noises, mothers spend late evenings stitching up realistic dresses for 7-year olds to dance in and money wasted in making that 17th century style cabinet out of MFI flatpack that sits in the corner of a darkened stage. Be creative! With a little bit of imagination you can create some quite stunning imagery with chairs, tables and even actors!

I once saw an excellent children's piece done out of a wardrobe by Visible Fictions. Children sat and believed because they wanted to. The strength of the characters and the acting enchanted and enriched the young audience. As the director you have to be careful you're not dragged into workshops to deliberate over caster sizes whilst Johnnie in the chorus can't remember his last line and hearing him getting bawled at because 'he doesn't realise how much work goes into all of this and everyone else seems able to manage'. The next week everyone tut tuts as Johnny the dyslexic can't turn up for rehearsals.

One of my proudest achievements took three excellent actors, nine masks, a table and an easel. 100 per cent of schools it visited, and it visited nearly 100, thought it worked well or very well. It was simple, clear and what we didn't have we mimed. Nobody stood up and shouted, 'there's no table there!'

Posture

When asking someone to perform solo remember that they may not be vocally trained. Teach them to stand feet apart, evenly balanced on both feet with their chin slightly raised pointing their voices out towards the back of the hall. This is for recitals and not acting *please*. There is nothing worse than seeing ten kids standing beautifully poised having a conversation whilst none of them look at each other.

Posture is something which needs to be taught through practice. They won't learn nor truly understand what is being asked of them if you stand 20 feet away from them and shout at them. 'Stand up straight for God's sake!', terrifies people particularly me. Show them how to stand, learn vocal exercises, teach them to them, practice with them. Don't expect good habits without the rehearsal. A good book for this is Michael McCallion's *Voice Book*.

Rehearse Everything

And I mean everything—particularly the bow at the end. You may or may not believe that they can't bow but if you don't cover how to bow until the last rehearsal you'll see an entire cast falling over one another ducking heads at different times and to different sections of the audience. They then fall over each other as they try to get off-stage.

Equally important is to rehearse the technical details - any lighting, scene changes, music or whatever—well in advance of your performance. Planning and setting time aside to *discuss properly* what is done with the music on page 4 is just as necessary as rehearsing the words on page 4. Rehearse and learn. One of the most hilarious examples of how carefully rehearsing something can change its impact, was watching the Scots actor Andy Gray in Dario Fo's *Trumpets and Raspberries*. He had to mime opening a window. The stage manager would play street noises, cars etc. whilst he did this, thus the illusion without the window frame. Due to good rehearsal timing and the fact that they'd probably done the play 30 times, they had established a wee routine with the actor opening, shutting, opening, shutting the window as if to catch the stage manager out. (He never did—or was he ever trying to?) Because of the intimacy of his relationship to the audience—they loved it **and** had there been a mistake would have loved it even more particularly as Andy Gray's knack of playing the clown was so effective.

By rehearsing the technical details it can look so much more polished.

Ignore Old Wives Tales

My favourite dramatic tradition (which thoroughly upsets me) is **Don't turn your back on the audience**. I try to imagine an actor in the round delivering his lines like an ice skater to an audience who is trying to work out why Shakespeare on skates was thought necessary. It is common sense that if someone is loud enough and needs to turn 'upstage' that they will naturally turn their backs without losing any impact. It is also equally common sense that if they speak like a mouse in a paper bag they should always face their listeners.

There are a few other theatrical 'conventions' worth looking at because they do help make life easier as a director.

Masking is where one person stands in front of another, thus creating a 'mask' through which an audience can't see someone else. If your actors learn how not to mask and spend some time being reminded about it, it helps immeasurably when you are producing a play and the actors balance the stage for you.

Evil enters from the left' is an old tradition still held to especially in panto. Up to you what you do with it but I like to make my baddies appear from anywhere.

Stage right is the actor's right. Endless confusion reigns as you ask someone to go left when you mean right. To avoid this stage directions are always from the actor's perceptions.

The following diagram may help:

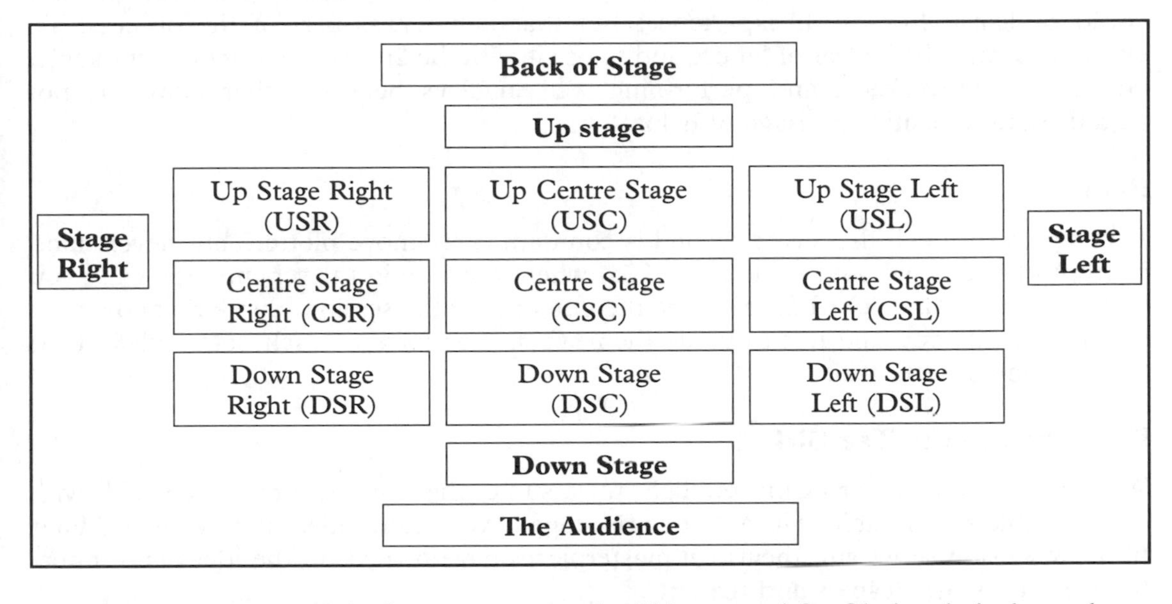

If someone exits stage left, the next entrance should be stage right. Obviously it depends on where the first is going and from where the last come **but** it does help to balance a stage and avoids everything coming from one side and therefore bumping into each other.

Always use upstage limbs. If standing sideways stretch out with the hand/leg closest to the back of the stage. It avoids partial masking, looks better and also helps unless you have a right-handed person trying to always use their left hand. Then perhaps getting them to go to the other side is better.

Always cross behind the people rather than walking in front of them. This can help but can be hilarious if someone down stage right has a coat to collect down stage left but must pass someone on an empty stage who is centre stage. They walk round that person when it would clearly be better to walk straight in front of them to collect the coat. Once again a theatrical convention to be tempered by common sense.

What'll I do with my hands? Ignore them. You do all day until someone asks you to do something and then suddenly from being these rather handy items which help you to communicate they suddenly become a demonic plague. The question is not what to do with them but why the actors' focus of attention is on them rather than anything else. The main reason why they have problems with their hands is that they tend to spend several weeks trying to act with a script superglued to them! If they are able to put the script down as soon as is possible by the time that they come to perform then they won't have a 'hand problem'.

Positively Fail

Like many dramatists I used to take my failures and the pain and anguish and ignore them. I would blame the audience for not understanding, the stage manager for not having the set ready, even the actors for not being good enough. This was equally true in workshops where I would attempt to forget the bad ones.

Then I realised how foolish I was being as I was not only ignoring the lessons that could be learnt from such experiences but that failure was part of the process. To embrace positively the fear of failure and to use it with the group to extract the workable, change the unworkable and performing well involves believing that failure is not negative but a positive message of help.

Plan

Don't plan so much that every second is counted, every move plotted, but never stand in front of people without some idea of (a) where they are in the scheme; (b) what you want to achieve and (c) what might be the outcome of the session. Similarly allow your group to guide you and not to guide them when they have a much better idea of (a) above than you ever will.

Don't Ignore the Tea Girl

We must never be arrogant enough to assume that the snotty nosed kid with questionable social habits will not at some stage have a better idea than we will. Major films, television series and theatrical masterpieces have turned on the ideas and inputs from electricians, cleaners and tea girls.

There are always, however, times when you are short of some genuine material which stops you from doing the work that you want to do.

Get Permission

Now earlier I mentioned the various types of performance that you can contemplate. Let me deal quickly with pre-written texts (*Grease*, *Return to the Forbidden Planet*, *Bugsy Malone*, *Annie*, *Oliver* etc.). Before you start *any* rehearsals you *must* have the written permission of the people who hold the copyright. The two largest holders of copyright for amateur performances are French's and Warner Chappell. Their addresses are listed in the Epilogue. They both do massive play lists and its well worthwhile sending for their catalogues. Each play commands a fee which is usually 15 per cent of gross box office **or** a straight amount. Be aware of how much you'll be paying before you start rehearsing!

Again the beauty of improvised performances is that you'll owe nobody money for using your own group's ideas. To help I have reproduced some improvised topics which can be put into workshops but were used in various settings which lead to performances. Now if you didn't want a full script these provide a few ideas on specific themes to get you started.

A Word About Rehearsing . . .

Flippantly I referred to 'rehearsals' earlier. What do you do in rehearsals? What do you do in the 'first' rehearsal? How do you cast your play? I can only explain what I do and hope it helps. So taking the last question first, here goes.

How Do You Cast?

I don't hold auditions. I find that they teach me nothing and ignore the learning process involved in productions and they debilitate people's abilities and heighten their anxieties. It also doesn't check on a key element—their ability to work with other people. You behave snootily once and you are dragged to reality every time you attend a rehearsal. I want a blend of people. The right people. What I want to produce is a show with a believable story-line, a comfortable cast and strong performances. All three came from being straight and sensible with the cast and with knowing them.

Firstly you want believability. A 14-year old won't look like the mother of a 21-year old who wants to marry a 9-year old! (Unless of course the 14 and 9-year old look ancient and the 21-year old still gets a half-fare on the buses!) You want people to believe in the *look* of a production. So consider that first.

Secondly if a musical, cast those that can sing, if a dance show cast those that can dance. I will have workshopped together with a group for some time before a show. I get to know them just before I cast them. Once I think I have the right blend, I think I'm ready for the first rehearsal. If I need to know what people's abilities are I will give them a form to fill in. Finally why not ask them what *they* want to play?

What Do You Do at the Very First Rehearsal?

A lot of people have 'a read through'. Everyone sits and tries out the parts. Some people use the read through as an audition process. However, people read things cold and it may be a two-and-a-half hour show. That's a long time to sit and read for. It is also quite disparaging if you're dyslexic or a slow reader. I like to workshop the story using key elements as cliffhangers. I like to do that before I cast so that everyone knows the story-line before we begin rehearsals. The first rehearsals *ought* to be interesting and **not** boring. One point to remember however is to try to make sure that everyone who needs a script leaves with a script. (Getting them to bring them back is quite another story.)

What Do You Do in Rehearsals?

Be organised. There is firstly a great temptation to start every rehearsal at page 1. **Don't.** We have youth theatre weekly set times (Saturday mornings 9.30 a.m.–11.00 a.m.). *Everyone* attends at that time weekly and we do whole group scenes and give out information for the coming weeks. We begin rehearsals weekly on a Saturday, extending to 1.00 p.m. or 4.00 p.m., then start Sundays, then weekdays, then whole weekends and weekday evenings. I tell them to cancel life for the week before production and the week of production.

We start at the first rehearsal with an advance schedule alerting parents of days when we will call rehearsals. We then organise rehearsals to suit. I have enclosed a typical schedule. Don't wait until the first night, see who turns up and ask 'well what can we do'? Call rehearsals, allocate times for things and set up the play. A production plan is usually in our Administration Folder and The Book. It helps to plan. If you plan well ahead and properly you look efficient **and** you can achieve greatness according to somebody famous.

Are there any Legal Things to be Aware Of

Yes and no. Amateur performances are not governed by legislation, however performances involving a fee are. Apart from the licence payment and permission for the script there may be no other things legally to consider. However should your little darling become a little darling professionally then contact your local education authority with regards to children's performance licences. These are vital and it is illegal not to have one under certain strict circumstances. You will need parental and school permission for absences from school and these are covered in the forms. Days off from school for your rehearsals may be frowned upon so check up with school and parents *before* you consider doing them.

ACT TWO, SCENE 4
THE PRODUCER'S CHECKLIST

The following sheets make into a handbook which will help with your initial planning.

For this play

Title of the play:
Producer: ______________________________

Author: ______________________________

Director: ______________________________

Stage manager: ______________________________

Administrator: ______________________________

For this performance

Dates: Venues:
____

Technical team

Musical director: ______________________________

Choreographer: ______________________________

Deputy stage manager: ______________________________

Assistant stage manager: ______________________________

Group:

P—Producer ______________

CHOR—Choreographer ______________

D—Director ______________

MD—Musical director ______________

A—Administrator ______________

PM—Production manager ______________

SM—Stage manager ______________

DSM—Deputy stage manager ______________

ASM—Assistant stage manager ______________

Pre-rehearsal

Week 1	**Week beginning: __________**
Play agreed	P/D
Budget finalised	P/D
Personnel appointed	P/D
Venues finalised for performance	P/A
Research begun	TEAM
Project plan completed	PM
Admin folders set up	A
First rehearsal finalised	D

Week 2—Administration meeting	**Week beginning: __________**
Arrange rehearsals; book venues	A
Rehearsal schedule drawn up	D/A

Pre-production

Week 3—Production meeting	**Week beginning: __________**
Production meeting 1	D/DM/CHOR/SM/M/PM/P/A
Rehearsal schedule weeks 2–6 issued	A/D
Posters and leafleting decisions	A/P
Cast the show and measure them	D/PM

Week 4	**Week beginning: __________**
Rewrites discussed	P/D/CHOR/MD
Venues contacted again re timetable	PM/SM
Check on venues for performances	P/D/PM/SM
Music discussed	D/MD
Venues contacted re requirements	P/PM

Week 5	**Week beginning: __________**
The book ready	SM/ASM
Props list version 1	SM/DSM
Production meeting 2	D/TEAM
Open booking	A

Week 6	**Week beginning: __________**
Posters and leaflets deadline	P
History/biogs for programme	P/D
Technical requirements list	D/PM/SM
Budget checked	P/D

Week 7	**Week beginning:** ________________
Set list for stage manager	P/PM/SM
Props list version 2	PM/SM
Week 8	**Week beginning:** ________________
Deadline for set design	DM
Rehearsal props bought and introduced	SM/ASM
Production meeting 3	P
Week 9	**Week beginning:** ________________
Set building	SM/DSM
Poster/leaflet distribution	A
Run off invite list to be checked	A/P
Week 10	**Week beginning:** ________________
Building of set continues	SM/DSM
Press release	D/P/A
Programme copy ready	A/P/D
Invites out	A/P
Check props list	D/PM/SM/DSM
Final bookings checked	P
Production meeting whole staff	D/P
Week 11	**Week beginning:** ________________
Build and paint set	SM/DSM
Design lighting	SM/DSM/ASM
Organise stage crew	SM/D
Letter to parents	P
Week 12	**Week beginning:** ________________
Run lighting	SM/DSM
Run stage crew	SM/PM
Press release/photo-call	P/D/A
Technical rehearsal	P/SM/DSM/ASM
Production meeting	P
Allocate dressing rooms	P/SM

Production

Week 13

Day 1: ____________________________

Production meeting whole staff	P
Record keeping	SM
Planning of returns	PM/SM
Run (lighting/curtain/stage crew/the show)	SM/DSM/ASM
Running repairs	SM/DSM/ASM
Setting up/striking show	SM/DSM/ASM
Strike set and rearrange venue as it was before	SM/DSM/ASM

Day 2: ______________________________	
Run (lighting/curtain/stage crew/the show)	SM
Running repairs	SM
Setting up/striking show	SM
Strike set and rearrange venue as it was before	SM
Day 3: ______________________________	
Run (lighting/curtain/stage crew/the show)	SM
Running repairs	SM
Setting up/striking show	SM
Strike set and rearrange venue as it was before	SM
Day 4—Dress rehearsal: _______________	
Dress rehearsal	D
Run (lighting/curtain/stage crew/the show)	SM
Running repairs	SM
Setting up/striking show	SM
Strike set and rearrange venue as it was before	SM
Show report	SM
Notes to cast	D
Day 5—Opening: ______________________	
Audience figures	P/A
Run (lighting/curtain/stage crew/the show)	SM
Running repairs	SM
Setting up/striking show	SM
Strike set and rearrange venue as it was before	SM
Show report	SM
Notes to cast	D
Report	SM
Day 6—Close: _________________________	
Audience figures	P/A
Run (lighting/curtain/stage crew/the show)	SM
Running repairs	SM
Setting up/striking show	SM
Strike set and rearrange venue as it was before	SM
Show report	SM
Notes to cast	D
Report	SM
Collect scripts	SM/D

Post-production

Week 14	**Week beginning: ____________**
Returns	D/PM/SM
Post-mortem	P/D
Final record keeping	P
Week 15	**Week beginning: ____________**
Assessment	P/D

In the order to which they are referred in the handbook here come the sample items.

- Registration Form.
- Signing in Sheet.
- Production Plan—*Twelfth Night.*
- Advance Notice Schedule weeks 1–16—*Return to the Forbidden Planet.*
- Rehearsal Schedule—*Young Frankenstein.*
- Costume/Character Sheet.
- The Book.
- Notes for Parents About the Final Week of Rehearsals—*Return to the Forbidden Planet.*
- Biography Sheet.
- Future productions for this year.
- A Press Release.
- A Programme.
- A Show Report—*The Lion, The Witch and The Wardrobe.*

Registration Form

Name of youth theatre: ______________________________ Date: ________

Name: ____

School: ____ Year: ____________

Address: ____

____

____ Post code: ___________

Home tel. no: _________________________________ Date of Birth: ______

Name of emergency contact: ____

Relationship (aunt/granny etc.) Tel. no: ___________________________

Note: This is very basic information. You may also want to include medical/dietary conditions you should be made aware of when you have them for over 3–4 hours. If you are contemplating ever having them off school a photocopy of their birth certificate and two passport size photographs requested now would be advantagous.

Signing in Sheet

Name		Date	Matinee In	Matinee Out	Evening In	Evening Out

Note: This simple self ticking registration form is handy when parents turn up or there is a practice fire alarm.

Production Plan
Twelfth Night

Scene	Place	Character	Done	Props/Lighting/Scenery
Act one				
One	Orsinos' palace	Orsino Curio Valentine Lords Servants	Y	(Suitable props, lighting effects and scenery should be listed here)
Two	Shore	Viola Captain Sailors	Y	
Three	Olivia's house	Sir Toby Belch Maria Sir Andrew Aguecheek Servants	Y	

Note: You want to continue this throughout the play so that you may group regearsals round people. Foe example Shakespeare runs various storylines. If, in *Twelfth Night*, you can get the same people together on one night you could concentrate heavily on say 4–5 scenes. However your minor characters need to be called and your stage crew need to know what props etc. to bring.

Advance Notice Schedule Weeks 1–16
Return to the Forbidden Planet

Date	Week number	Notes
Sat 3rd January	One	Return after the holiday and 9.30 a.m.–11 a.m. for all
Sat 10th January	Two	
Wed 14th January		
Sat 17th January	Three	
Wed 21st January		
Sat 24th January	Four	
Wed 28th January		Likely booking night
Sat 31st January	Five	
Sun 1st February		Start of Sunday rehearsals
Wed 4th February		
Sat 7th February	Six	
Sun 8th February		
Wed 11th February		
Sat 14th February	Seven	
Sun 15th February		
Wed 18th February		
Sat 21st February	Eight	
Sun 22nd February		
Wed 25th February		
Sat 28th February	Nine	
Sun 1st March		
Wed 4th March		
Sat 7th March	Ten	
Sun 8th March		
Wed 11th March		
Sat 14th March	Eleven	
Sun 15th March		
Mon 16th March		First Monday rehearsal
Wed 18th March		
Sat 21st March	Twelve	
Sun 22nd March		
Mon 23rd March		
Wed 25th March		
Sat 28th March	Thirteen	
Sun 29th March		
Mon 30th March		
Tues 31st March		First Tuesday rehearsal
Wed 1st April		
Sat 4th April	Fourteen	Last two weeks
Sun 5th April		
Mon 6th April		
Tues 7th April		
Wed 8th April		

Sat 11th April	Fifteen	
Sun 12th April		
Mon 13th April		
Tues 14th April		
Wed 15th April		
Thurs 16th April		
Fri 17th April		
Sat 18th April	Sixteen	
Sun 19th April		
Mon 20th April		
Tues 21st April		
Wed 22nd April		Get in at the Gaiety
Thurs 23rd April		Tech rehearsal at the Gaiety
Fri 24th April		Open at the Gaiety
Sat 25th April		2 performances—matinee and evening Gaiety

Rationale: At the beginning of any rehearsal period you need to be precisely clear how much time you will be rehearsing for. For many—including yourself—it can be quite a shock. It's not the first time someone has turned up at a Dress Rehearsal fully expecting to be at the front of the chorus when they haven't ever been at any of the other rehearsals

Rehearsal Schedule
Young Frankenstein

Day	Date	Time	To be rehearsed		Location	Cast
Tuesday	8th October	7.30 p.m.– 9.30 p.m.	Songs			Whole Youth Theatre
Wednesday	9th October	7.30 p.m.– 9.30 p.m.	Act one	Four	Railway station	Elizabeth Freddy Frankenstein Conductor Crowd
				Five	Railway carriage	Conductor Freddy Frankenstein Boy Egor Inga Frau Blucher
				Twelve	Laboratory	Freddy Frankenstein Egor
				Thirteen	Brain depository	Egor
				Fourteen	Laboratory	Inga Egor Freddy Frankenstein
Saturday	12th October	9.30 a.m.– 11.00 a.m.	Act one	Fifteen	Meeting hall	1st elder 1st villager 2nd villager 2nd elder 3rd villager Inspector Kemp Crowd
		11.00 a.m.– 12.30 p.m.	Act two	Twelve	Meeting hall	Inspector Kemp Crowd
				Fourteen	Outside castle	Inspector Kemp Crowd Freddy Frankenstein Egor
				Fifteen	Outside castle	Egor Freddy Frankenstein Elizabeth Monster Crowd

Day	Date	Time	To be rehearsed		Location	Cast
Saturday	12th October	12.30 p.m.– 1.00 p.m.	SCLC meeting			
		1.00 p.m.– 1.30 p.m.	Committee meeting			
		1.30 p.m.– 2.30 p.m.	Act one	Sixteen	Laboratory	Freddy Frankenstein Inga Egor Monster
				Seventeen	Laboratory	Inspector Kemp Freddy Frankenstein Inga
				Eighteen	Laboratory	Frau Blucher Monster Freddy Frankenstein Inga

Note: At the beginning of any rehearsal period you need to be exactly clear on how much time you will rehearse for. For many it can be quite a shock! It's not the first time that some little darling turned up at the Dress Rehearsal expecting to perform every dance routine for the next three nights.

You are amalgamating your production plan with your advance schedule and thus making sure everyone knows *exactly* what's happening when. You can hand it out or pin it on the wall.

Costume/Character Sheet

Performance ______________________

Character ______________________

Actor ______________________

Stage manager ______________________

Garment	Size	Description	Source	Got?
Hat				
Shirt				
Jumper/cardigan				
Socks				
Shoes				
Accessories				
Props				

The Book

<table>
<tr><td rowspan="4">Lighting cues</td><td colspan="3">Page</td><td rowspan="4">Sound cues</td></tr>
<tr><td colspan="3">Stage at start of page</td></tr>
<tr><td>Scenery notes</td><td>Costume notes</td><td>Props notes</td></tr>
<tr><td colspan="3">Stage at end of page</td></tr>
</table>

Notes for Parents About the Final Week of Rehearsals

Return to the Forbidden Planet

Dear Parents
As we enter the final week of rehearsals there are one or two issues which we need to highlight for the benefit of the weans in the week ahead.

What is the timetable?

Timetable			
Monday 20th April	6.00 p.m.–10.00 p.m.	Whole Youth Theatre	Gaiety Theatre*
Tuesday 21st April	6.00 p.m.–10.00 p.m.	Whole Youth Theatre	Gaiety Theatre
Wednesday 22nd April	6.00 p.m.–10.00 p.m.	Whole Youth Theatre	Gaiety Theatre
Thursday 23rd April	6.00 p.m.–10.00 p.m.	Whole Youth Theatre	Gaiety Theatre
Friday 24th April	6.00 p.m.–10.00 p.m.	Whole Youth Theatre	Gaiety Theatre
Saturday 25th April	1.00 p.m.–5.00 p.m.	Whole Youth Theatre	Gaiety Theatre
	6.00 p.m.–10.00 p.m.	Whole Youth Theatre	Gaiety Theatre

*I am trying to sneak into the Gaiety to get onto the stage on Monday night but may not be able to do so. I will tell the cast for definite on Monday but this might be at the Civic.

The most frequently asked questions.

Do they need to be at every rehearsal?
Strictly speaking yes. However I am no ogre. If there are genuine reasons as to why someone cannot make it then they will of course be let off. The last week is the toughest because there are a lot of things where we need to take it over and over and over again. Imagine our frustration when we have spent hours doing something and then find that someone was missing that night and we have to do it all over again! (It has happened.)

Isn't that asking too much of the younger ones?
Possibly, yes. This is one reason why I won't take them in at younger than nine. We have several 'little darlings' of 5,6 and 7 thrust at us as the most talented children in the world. By now it would be abuse mentally and physically to ask them to complete a timetable like the one above so we don't let them in the door in the first place. If your 9 or 10 or 11-year old is finding it tough let me know and we shall allow them time off to recover.

Can they take time off school?
Strictly speaking no. There have been instances where young people have been given a day or two to recover because they have been exhausted and going to school would be too much for them. Many people feel that a day or two wouldn't do too much

harm. However I can't condone school absences and have to leave it to your own conscience!

What do they need to bring with them?
They need a snack at the interval. By now you may have been dispatched round Safeway for bananas. It's the best energy food and I've advised them against sugary snacks like chocolate. (I don't take my own advice sometimes!) Apart from that they will need to bring their own costumes and any props that they have been given to bring in.

Do you need any help?
I'll let you know. We don't need help often as the youth theatre operates a policy of self-help and the young people will be given the responsibility to do something rather than trying to find a volunteer. Also I find it so so hard to find jobs for volunteers because the young people do so much. Don't think that I'm not grateful, I am very grateful, but we'll let you know!

What happens at 6 p.m.?
The young people are 'called' for one-and-a-half hours before curtain up. They enter the building and 'sign in'. Half an hour after the 'call time' the assistant stage manager checks the sheet and anyone not in is phoned to find out where they are. If there are good reasons why someone cannot get in by 6 p.m. they need to let us know in advance by telling Arlene (assistant producer) or Claire (stage manager). At 6.30 p.m. we assemble on-stage and warm-up. We take them through a physical, vocal and mental warm-up. At this point we give 'notes' about the previous performance or anything worth noting that they have or have not been doing. 7.00 p.m. they are sent to starting positions and we are ready for an audience. At curtain down they have to go to their dressing rooms tidy it and **then** leave. (That includes the boys!) On Sunday this is adjusted for the matinee with a 'call' at 1.00 p.m..

Please, please note that there is no youth theatre that morning!!

Are there still tickets?
Yes. You can buy them at the box office during the week. We have few left for the Saturday evening but lots for the matinee.

What's this programme thing?
We have for the first time ever spent a considerable amount of money printing a full programme. It will cost £2. This is because we need to make the money back on it. The cast will not see the final thing until the Friday evening and I would urge you to buy it when you come to see the show because they will not come home with one tucked under their arms. The programme is a youth theatre brochure, which is being sent to every casting director and agent in the country after the show.

Anything else?
Projekt 11:92 have indicated that they would like to run a weekly class in Ayr and judging by the reaction this looks as though it would be very popular. I shall questionnaire everyone soon as the workshops would have to cost to cover them. If anyone has any thoughts in the meantime then let me have them.

In the meantime thanks for your help and patience and here's to the biggest Youth theatre show ever!

Aye Yours,

Donald C. Stewart
Youth Theatre Organiser

Note: The final weeks are unlike any other. They can be highly stressful and you'll snap. Be prepared and this handy list of things to consider allows you to concentrate on the important things whilst parents/children read.

Biography sheet

Role you played	Year	Play/Production	Company
Were you an actor/ producer etc. and if an actor who were you?	199 what?	Name of the show	Who was responsible for it—school? Dance school? Or who?

I normally stick this on the back of the Registration Form so that I can write up simple biographies in the programme. It's a little better than just listing their names and characters.

Future productions for this year

Play/Production	Company

Press Release

Youth Theatre's Trip into Space is Set to Land

For Immediate Release

Contact: Donald C. Stewart—Your Tempest Tour Rep

We are delighted to announce that the Great and Mighty Zog, wanted on all 13 sides of the Universe shall be appearing alongside her menacing gang Hell's Aliens at the Gaiety Theatre on Friday 24th and Saturday 25th April. The town of Ayr were first to see the Mighty Zog, universal criminal mastermind, when she went on walkabout round Ayr last Saturday.

You can catch the Great and Mighty Zog along with 100 other young people in the Youth Theatre's largest ever production at the Gaiety Theatre. ***Return to the Forbidden Planet*** by Bob Carlton appears courtesy of Warner Chappell and includes such favourites as *Monster Mash*, *The Shoop Shoop Song* and *Great Balls of Fire*. Tickets are still available priced £5/£3 from the Gaiety Theatre Box Office (01292) 611222 and this represents the first collaboration between Musical Director Bud Greenwood of Troon, Youth Theatre Organiser Donald C Stewart and Projekt 11:92 of Glasgow.

Apart from over 100 young people being involved the Youth Theatre has produced a full colour programme which includes individual photographs and CV's. Once the curtain falls on the production the programmes shall be sent off to casting directors throughout the UK to hopefully begin some illustrious careers. Production of the programme has been possible thanks to the kindness and generosity of local businesses.

Note to Editors: The Youth Theatre shall be rehearsing each evening in the Gaiety this week from 6 p.m. to 10 p.m. and we would welcome the opportunity for group photographs to be taken.

Note: You want publicity so advertise. Local newpapers in particular, are quite good at putting in editorial for local groups.

A Programe

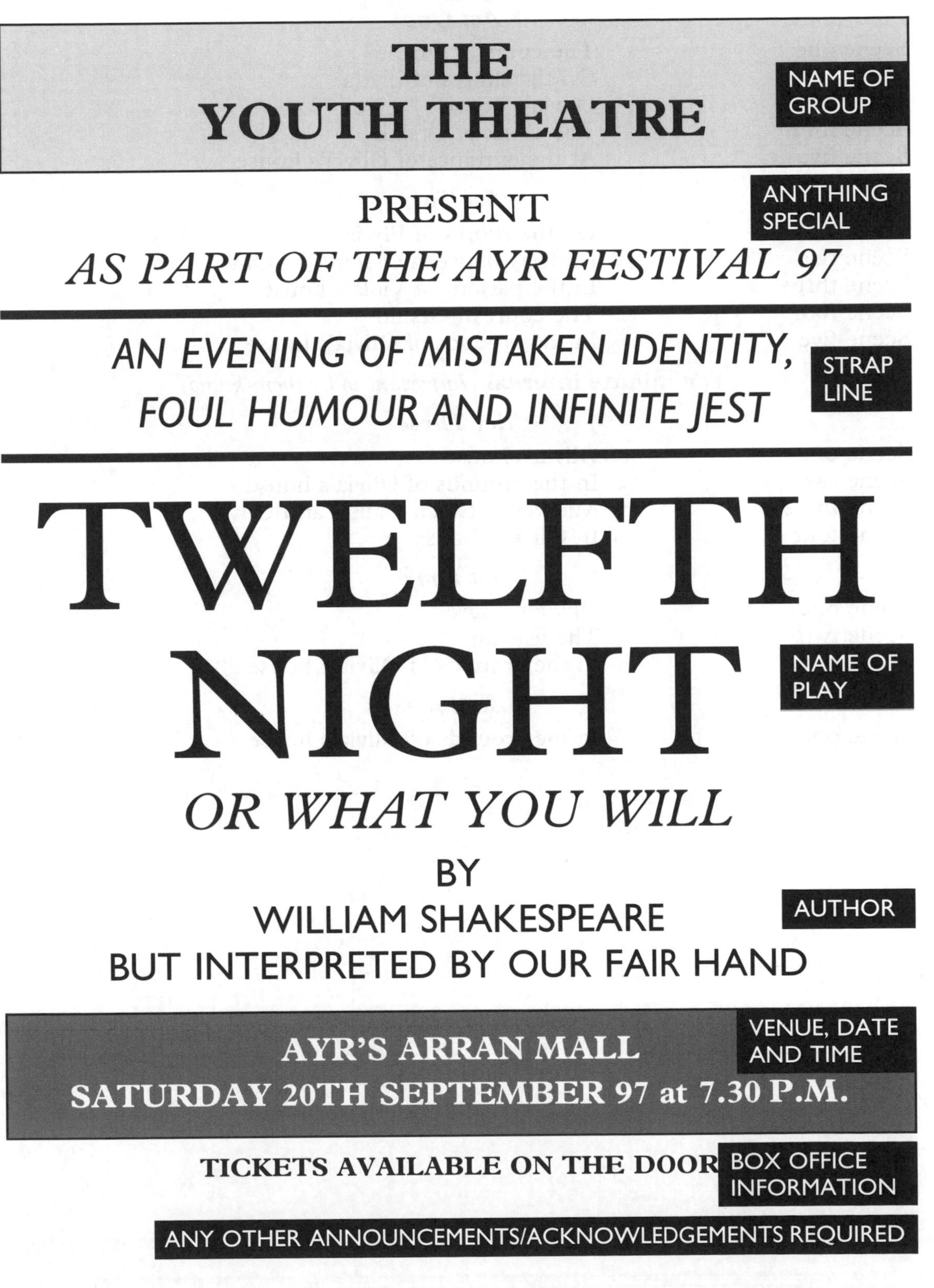
THE
YOUTH THEATRE
NAME OF GROUP
PRESENT
ANYTHING SPECIAL
AS PART OF THE AYR FESTIVAL 97
AN EVENING OF MISTAKEN IDENTITY,
FOUL HUMOUR AND INFINITE JEST
STRAP LINE
TWELFTH
NIGHT
NAME OF PLAY
OR WHAT YOU WILL
BY
WILLIAM SHAKESPEARE
AUTHOR
BUT INTERPRETED BY OUR FAIR HAND
AYR'S ARRAN MALL
SATURDAY 20TH SEPTEMBER 97 at 7.30 P.M.
VENUE, DATE AND TIME
TICKETS AVAILABLE ON THE DOOR
BOX OFFICE INFORMATION
ANY OTHER ANNOUNCEMENTS/ACKNOWLEDGEMENTS REQUIRED

List of Scenes (*Usually helpful for the audience*)

Act One

Scene one	The court of Orsino
Scene two	On the shores of Illyria
Scene three	Olivia's house
Scene four	The court of Orsino
Scene five	At the entrance of Olivia's house

Act Two

Scene one	On the shores of Illyria
Scene two	Midway between Orsino and Olivia
Scene three	In the parlour of Viola's house
Scene four	The court of Orsino
Scene five	In the grounds of Olivia's house

Ten minute interval (*Important to let them know*)

Act Three

Scene one	Olivia's house
Scene two	In the grounds of Olivia's house
Scene three	Midway between Orsino and Olivia
Scene four	In Olivia's house

Act Four

Scene one	Olivia's house
Scene two	The asylum
Scene three	In the grounds of Olivia's house

Act Five

Scene one	In the grounds of Olivia's house

The Production Team

(Here's where the biographies help)

Donald C. Stewart
Producer
Previously Director of Community Education at Borderline Theatre where he ran Scotland's largest Community Network of Community Arts for nearly five years. Donald has been Youth Theatre Organiser for South Ayrshire's award winning Youth Theatre for three years as well as Business Development Officer at The Scottish Child Law Centre. Donald has produced in excess of 30 plays for young people and had his work presented on the BBC, ITV and Channel 4. He is working on his first book *Youth Work and Drama* at the present time and one of his plays is to be produced by the Canadian Troubadours Theatre Company, Toronto. Donald has also worked in TV and film with the National Lottery advert, *Rob Roy* and *Braveheart* to his credit.

Arlene McCreadie
Assistant producer/Maria, Olivia's waiting gentlewoman
Arlene has been with the company for only two years and yet in that time she has performed, played in a band, assisted as a director and directed for Mayfest. Credits as an actor/musician include *Alice* (BYTz), *Macbeth* (Borderline Community Group), *The Nest Egg* (SAYT), *The Toybox* (Reid Kerr College), *Juno and the Paycock* (Reid Kerr College), *Young Frankenstein* (SAYT), *The Water is Wild* (Borderline Community Group), *Tam O'Shanter* (SAYT) and *Taggart* (STV—twice!). As a director Arlo has worked on *A Guid Catch for Mayfest 97* and the Dramattack Summer production of *Fablespake*.

Alex Henderson
Assistant director/assistant stage manager
Alex has stage managed before for the youth theatre in *The Lion the Witch and the Wardrobe*. We have him on loan as he is also appearing in the Belmont Academy production of *Gregory's Girl* at the beginning of October in the Civic.

Colin Johnston
Assistant director
Another one on loan who is appearing in *Gregory's Girl*, Colin made an incredible debut for SAYT in their biggest selling show in years when he appeared as Edmund in *The Lion, the Witch and the Wardrobe*. Previously Colin had played Barrington in Belmont Academy's *Maid Marion and Her Merry Friends*.

The Crew *(Don't forget any of them!)*

Simon Plummeridge
Production manager
Simon has been working in all aspects of theatre from touring Europe and Scandinavia to working with the BBC and ITV with Eugene's flying ballet. He has worked with various companies in Scotland such as Fablevision, Scottish Youth Theatre and now SAYT. He spent many years working with Youth, Community and Special Needs Art.

Claire Allison
Stage manager
Claire's stage management has seen her work as production manager for the Mayfest productions and take charge of props for the Kilmarnock College production of *Albert*.

Stewart Graham
Assistant stage manager
From appearing with AAOC in *Oliver Stewart* landed a role in *Peter Pan* at the Gaiety. Stewart then joined the youth theatre where he quickly made an impression as Aslan in *The Lion, the Witch and the Wardrobe*.

The Cast (*In order of appearance makes it democratic*)

Jonathon Ross
Orsino, Duke or Count of Illyria
This is Jonathon's second SAYT show with a memorable appearance as the gormless Igor in the World Premiere of *Young Frankenstein* behind him. Following on from that was his first panto at the Gaiety in *Peter Pan*. With Ayr Academy Jonathon was First Hood in *Sugar*.

Alison Gehring
Olivia, a countess
Alison is a veritable newcomer to the youth theatre making her debut as so many did in the Mayfest tour of 97. This is her first major Shakespearean role and we are relishing her performance.

Kevin Williamson
Sebastian, brother to Viola
Kevin's cartoons seem to have been as ever present in the youth theatre as Kevin himself. His debut came in *Tam O'Shanter* with further performances as Mr Hilltop and Jack Spratt in *Young Frankenstein*. Previously with Belmont Academy, Kevin was in *The Boyfriend* and played Robin Hood in *Maid Marion and Her Merry Friends*.

Amelia Geddes
Viola, sister to Sebastian
Having done quite a few of SAYT's conference performances this is Amelia's first major role. Amelia played in the band and on stage at *Young Frankenstein* but her ability to convey complex emotions on stage to hardened professionals brought her a more challenging role on this occasion.

Graham Hyslop
Sir Toby Belch, uncle to Olivia
From a hideous monster to Toby Belch! Who else but Graham. Graham has worked some memorable performances including a superbly gormless *Tam O'Shanter* and the frightening creation of one mad scientist in *Young Frankenstein*. Most memorable is Graham's scary rendition of the warm-up game—heads, shoulders, knees and toes!

Cameron Seaward
Malvolio, steward to Olivia
Cameron can lay claim to having worked with the producer sooner than anyone else in the cast—eight years ago in *Burns wizza Leprechaun!* And this is only the second time

they've worked together. Since then Cameron has performed in *Guys and Dolls* (Benny South Street), *Sugar* (Jerry/Daphne), and *Princess Ida* (the chancellor), as well as joining the cast of two Mayfest productions as a barman and the father of the bride.

Jess McCabe
Feste, a clown
Only her second youth theatre appearance after playing the mother in *Young Frankenstein*, Jess has also played some meaty roles at school including Alice in *Billy Liar*, MacDuff in *Macbeth*, and in the *Boyfriend* and *Annie Get your Gun*.

Kirsty Thompson
Fabian, servant to Olivia
From Alloway's *Joseph* and Belmont's *Ernie's Incredible Hallucinations*, Kirsty went on to play the Sheriff of Nottingham in *Maid Marion and Her Merry Friends* before performing with Ayrshire Voices in *Brigadoon* as May McGee. Kirsty's debut with SAYT was in the Mayfest production of *The Supervisor*.

Ryan Bharaj
Sir Andrew Aguecheek
Ryan was one of the original cast members from *Dracula Spectacula*. Since then he has established himself as one of the most well recognised faces of the youth theatre appearing up and down the country and constantly getting mixed up with his brother.

Susan McClelland
Valentine, gentleman attending on Orsino
There are still people who talk about Tallulah in *Bugsy Malone* and Susie's singing talents have marked her out. As Elizabeth in *Young Frankenstein* Susie's performance work hit a high spot. However this veteran of the stage had already managed to be in *Christmas Carol*, *Zigger Zagger* (mother), *Tam O'Shanter* (the innkeeper), *Telling Wilde Tales* (the mermaid), and *Beenie* (the supervisor). Susie made her directorial debut in Mayfest this year with *The Nest Egg*.

Susan Irving
Curio, gentleman attending on Orsino
This is Susan's first main show for SAYT. However her first appearance with the company came in the Mayfest shows this year as an outstanding newcomer as Betty in *The Supervisor*.

Jennifer Hainey
Antonio, a sea captain, friend to Sebastian
Jenny first performed with SAYT in *A Christmas Carol* way back in 1993. Since then her twin track career with both SAYT and the Borderline youth theatre have included *Summertime Blues* (Netty—BYTz), *Shanghaeid* (Morag—Borderline Theatre Co.), *Zigger Zagger* (head-teacher—AYT), *Bugsy Malone* (Louella—AYT), *Telling Wilde Tales* (the swallow—AYT), *Alice: The Musical* (Duchess—BYTz), *Tam O'Shanter* (Tamsin—SAYT) and the blind woman in SAYT's *Young Frankenstein.* Having passed her Workshop Training certificate with SAYT Jenny has also assisted in the direction of *The Incredible Vanishing* and *The Lion, the Witch and the Wardrobe* for SAYT.

Jenny Lindsay
Sea captain, friend to Viola
Jenny has performed with the youth theatre over many years and has managed to fit in the latest two full productions as well as many conference performances throughout the country.

Marion Lindsey
Priest
This is Marion's first production with the company having been flung the cassock only three weeks ago!

Lynn Barclay
First officer
Lynn's experience goes back several years to Borderline youth theatre's *Summertime Blues* where she played Letty. Since then she performed *Shanghaied* in a double bill alongside the author Liz Lochhead, *Zigger Zagger* (Glenice), *Bugsy Malone* (Captain Smolsky), *Tam O'Shanter* (chorus), *Young Frankenstein* (villager), *Alice: The Musical* (cook) and made her debut as assistant director in the Younger Group's *Incredible Vanishing.*

Lynne Porterfield
Second officer
Lynne has a tremendous amount of experience with the youth theatre amongst others. Her most recent foray onto the Gaiety stage was in the Amateur Opera's *Sound of Music.*

Gordon Taylor
Theatres manager
Gordon has never appeared in a production of *Twelfth Night* although he remembers one memorable production where his brother was in it which was the year after Freddie Boardley left the school!

Pamela Markwick
Youth theatre administrator
Pamela has never been in *Twelfth Night* either.

Robert Wilson
Administrative assistant
Just nae bother.

Special thanks to (*Anyone who's given money, props, costumes etc.*)
South Ayrshire Council (*Major funder*)
Jim Bryant and Alan McWhirter, The Ayr Festival 97, Northern Light, Mike Stewart, Fin, S.Y.T., Strategic Services, Borderline Theatre Co., British Ensign Estates and the fee paying public.

Special Note for Our Audience

This evening's performance in the open air will be upstanding. In Shakespeare's time there would have been few if any seats for the audience and we have sought to recreate that experience this evening. However, get up and move about and sit on the stages if you wish. This evening is designed to be both unique and enjoyed.

A Show Report

The Lion, The Witch and The Wardrobe
Friday 27th June 1997

Act One

We began the first act with the first ever full house that we have ever had. The first half of this act was very slick and professional. We had eventually cracked it. Despite the concentration slipping in the middle of it we can be proud that we recovered well and put in a cracking performance. I don't think there was a weak link on-stage.

The concentration slipped slightly backstage and crew had not read and therefore followed the detailed directions for act one scenes 9 to 12. Having said that they recovered very well indeed.

That all having been said, Jay you must remember your volume and particularly those in dressing room five have to learn to be quiet. The chorus must also remember to wait for their cues rather than spend their time trying to duck through the curtains to get on-stage first!

The build up to the interval was exceptionally atmospheric. The only disappointment was when we had the moving statues. They were bad enough but when someone is eating on-stage it bursts the blood vessels! However I was still very proud when the curtain came down.

Act Two

The Second Act followed at a cracking pace and we picked up the story and ran well with it. There were a few slip ups in the Second Act. This includes Cara—watch talking to your feet. You don't have to be worried about what you are supposed to say you learnt it so well.

Watch out for helping people on-stage. If people forget their lines someone saying '*Say the lines, say the lines*' sounds worse than a silence. If, in future someone doesn't say what they're supposed to then say the line for them!

When things are beginning to work so well just be careful that you do not start losing your concentration. People began to muddle their cues. Jodie check the sack before you go on-stage!

Watch noise off-stage which is distracting for those on-stage and the audience. Also watch where you put your ears if they fall off!

The pace of the Second Act was meant to keep the audience's attention and it did.

We know that there were more than a few excellent performances and Colin and Lynne were particularly effective. The tremendous feeling of tension that they managed on-stage is something from which we all should learn.

Note: Ask other members of the team to take turns at writing this up. The cast are always keen to find out how well they looked the night before. Conventionaly 'notes' from the director are verbally given before each performance from the previous evening's performance. A show report avoids having to stand and talk for 30 minutes and allows you to warm them up vocally instead. Yes Workshop Warm-ups do have a place!

ACT 2, SCENE 5
THE WRITER'S PORTFOLIO

Ideas for Improvised Performances

Showdown

James and John enter and look at each other across the room. The rest of the group scatter then decide to stop the showdown. James 'tigs' and downs each of the people he did in the game, except this time rather than in a frantic game it happens systematically one by one until their injuries litter the room. Just as James arrives at John for the showdown, James smiles, lifts his hand and switches to 'away' his remote control for his time machine and leaves.

Museum Games

One day George is taken to the museum with the school. Remembering how fascinating it was he decides to go back on his own. Unfortunately George arrives at the museum when it is due to shut. The curator, Rona, has shut up the museum for the night. All of the statues are around the museum and when Rona realises that someone is still in the museum she hunts and chases George down. When she finds George cowering in a corner George tells her why he's hiding in a museum and not at home . . .

Bully

In a quiet village a new order is announced. Soon a squad of new policemen will arrive to enforce the order. When they do arrive they seem sinister in their glasses which mark them out from the rest. Firstly four young people with similar hair disappear. One young girl protests publicly in the square and all are listening when the 'glasses' turn on her and take her out. Dramatically when they have finished they turn as one to confront the unfriendly village. They stand for a moment allowing the silence to descend before they . . .

Mice!

Number 12 Acacia Avenue has a mouse problem. The largest 'cat' is called in. Tigger saunters towards the mouse hole slowly and looks in. What he sees is a labyrinth of tunnels which he can just squeeze into. In he goes and sees the mouse! So easy! He turns and runs smack into a mirror. The sniggering behind him does not help his mood as he turns and navigates around the outer part of the labyrinth. Eventually he finds himself in the same passageway. Feeling cocky, Tigger pounces nearly catching the mouse on the turn. In the second passageway Tigger marks time realising that the mouse's legs will tire before his will. He is proven right as the mouse turns the fourth corner. Tigger rears up as he sees the mouse stop. With all his might Tigger pounces—right at that mirror!

Haunted House

A group of young kids pass by a haunted house every day without going in. One day they decide to approach it by walking up the path. They walk together slowly. Then one of them notices a shape at the window, they freeze. They move more cautiously till they see a bigger shape appear at the door. Again they freeze. The eldest Susan, who till now was at the back marches up to the front telling them not to worry as it is probably quite harmless. She turns to see a cat sauntering out of the house. After the initial shock they relax and laugh a little. Susan is now in front and turns to see an old man lunging towards her. Everyone screams and runs but the old man is quicker than Susan, grabs her and drags her into the house never to be seen again!

War Report

The war correspondent at the edge of the war between two villages reports on each village deciding which of their mythical missionaries to send in against their enemies. First time round both send their wizards who out-zap each other. One village stays with the wizards whilst the opposing village bring in their heavies, the giants. This is a terrible mistake as their opponents the Wizards clean up the battlefield. wizards, having been sent in twice on one side are sent in to clean up the rest. Sneakily their opponents have second guessed this strategy and have brought back the wizards. Their strategy is successful in making the sides even again. To prevent further bloodshed both sets of wizards are sent onto the battlefield to negotiate peace. The pixies on both sides mutter their discontent and announce the establishment of a pixie state. Both villages are incensed as both have sizeable pixie communities. The only state to recognise the pixie struggle are the likes of Iraq, Turkey and Iran.

Three Little Piggies

The three little children assemble to be told of their story by granny. The story loosely follows the three little piggies that went in search of the perfect house except in this version instead of the perfect house they go in search of the perfect family.

The plot

Scene one: Child number one is Cara who goes to her mother and father who are played by Amelia and Colin. She wants to be involved in the decisions in the house but is ignored by both her parents.

Scene two: Stewart is piggie number two whose father, Colin, is identified as the big bad wolf, listening to everything that Stewart asks for and then ignoring what he is told.

Scene three: Amelia is a single parent who listens to what her children are asking. She then explains what they will do after she has told them why or why not she is going to do what they want. When Colin the big bad wolf huffs and puffs they just don't let him in.

Health? Services

Scene one: Opening the performance and the child's right to be heard looks at the three basic principles. This is by looking at a school scene where a teacher seems to be talking about sex education and is embarrassed by what they're doing but turns out to be talking about the welfare principle in the Children's Act.

Scene two: A young person in a waiting room with their father. They go in to see their brother who is caught up between his mother and father as consent is required for the operation. He seeks 'divine' intervention until his parents come to their senses—but is it too late?

Scene three: Bedridden physically disabled father being rough on the son who cares for him. School telephones to complain about son not coming to school when the son was shopping for the father. Father and son start at each other then reach an uneasy compromise.

Scene 4: 14-year old pregnant girl has parents telephoned by doctor prior to being able to tell the news herself. Doctor believes that an emergency order may be needed at birth. Girl is only five months on and pressure is having an adverse effect on her. Question of which order may be most appropriate?

Bullying in Care

This was used as part of the Children's Rights conference for foster kids in South Lanarkshire in 1997. These were anti-bullying messages which were used as drafts for a video.

Kerry's story

There was only one girl involved. She said that she didn't like the fact that boys found me attractive and I was doing all right at school. She used to come in and call me names in front of people and tell them not to talk to me. It's hard to cope being so lonely with everyone looking at you. One night I woke up wet as if I'd wet myself but it was my pillow that was wet. Someone had poured water all over my bed and I was soaking. No one owned up to it and we couldn't prove who'd done it so they gave me a lock on my bedroom door and made sure there was someone extra on at night. But it was very difficult because everyone knew it was me that had been targeted.

Marc's story

I was in a unit with lots others. I wasn't one to mix with the others when they went out. This guy, Davy, was into giving me a hard time. He would shout at me and have a go in class. It kept on going when we went back to the living areas and then one night he went for me in the toilet because he knew that there wasn't anybody to see him. I went and told the staff who moved me into another class. They told everyone that I was being moved to somewhere so that I could be stretched with my school work. It did the trick and I didn't see Davy so often so he didn't have the chance to keep it going.

Diane's story

Interviewer *Where were you living at the time?*
Diane There were 17 others in the unit and I was the last one in.
Interviewer *Did you make friends?*

Diane Not really. There were some in the unit who shared with me but they had a go.

Interviewer *How do you mean?*

Diane There were three of them. Christine made the other two, Debbie and Maggie, take down the posters I had put up and started taking stuff out of the wardrobe that was mine and wore it.

Interviewer *Did you not object?*

Diane How?

Interviewer *Tell someone, a member of staff.*

Diane Fat lot of good that did.

Interviewer *Explain.*

Diane I said I was too sick to go to school and one of the staff twigged. She came to see me and had guessed what was going on. So I told her.

Interviewer *Everything?*

Diane Yes. She went and saw them and they denied it. Christine then got hold of me and kicked ma head in. Then they moved me. It took them until I was thumped before I was moved.

Ryan's story

It doesn't start with people doing it in front of teachers or that. It's normally when they've had to go out of the room. They can start by the chanting or the whispering behind you. It's like they're challenging everyone else in the room to see if anyone will stand up for me. When they don't then it can get physical or they just steal my stuff. Because they think I'm from another country they think they're superior to me. Once when the teacher came back in the room I nearly stood up and told him what had been happening but then someone asked him if he thought that England was going to win their football match against Germany and he said something about how the English didn't deserve to win anything so I didn't bother.

Greig's story

I'm only small. They started by telling me what to do because I was the youngest. When I told them where to get off they started teasing me about things I didn't understand. I got embarrassed about it because all I wanted was to be part of their gang—part of their unit. They wouldn't let me until I passed the Test. The Test was to steal some money from one of the staff. When I refused to do it they started telling people things about me and then they started to pick on me by tripping me up or playing rough games which looked fun to the staff. I didn't steal the money but they changed the game and I did the Test. I didn't tell anyone because I had just been taken from my last home and I didn't want to be taken from another one.

Performance Scripts

The following scripts are from short performances presented in a variety of settings throughout the UK. All came from improvisations before being written as scripts. They are copyright friendly!

Giving Young People a Voice

G Ladies and gentlemen, boys and girls we give you . . .
B The voice
[Jenny opens her mouth and nothing comes out. Barry and Graham look blank at each other]
B Graham
G Barry
B This is serious
G Indeed it is
B But don't panic
G I wasn't about to
B I'll send for a specialist
G You do that
B I will. Miss Geddes.
[Enter Amelia]
Am Mr McLean
B Miss Geddes
Am Mr Hyslop
G Miss Geddes
B The problem [*indicates Jenny*] is that this young person here . . .
G Has no voice
Am And?
B And . . . well . . . you see . . . we, that is . . .
G And I . . .
B We would like to give it a voice
G Well we could give it this one. See me. See birds, see me an birds and football. See me an football, see what am I doing here Barry?
B Making a complete . . . returning officer of yourself
Am It's quite clear what the problem is
B What?
Am You mean you can't see?
G He can see. The problem is we can't hear. [*To Barry*] Are you sure she knows what she's doing?
B She's the finest specialist in Dumfries
G I can see that but does she know what she's doing?
Am Gentlemen
G [*Looks about*] Has someone come in?
Am What this young person needs is to know that she can trust you
G Us?
B This is more serious than I thought

Am	She has to know that you are ready
G	For what?
Am	For her to express herself
B	But what do you mean?
Am	Are you two doing anything today?
G	See me . . . see birds . . .
Am	[*Looks at Jenny*] This is more serious than I thought [*Jenny nods*] Mr Hyslop, Mr McLean come with me and spend a day with young people
B and G	Do what?
J	Oh come on before you dry up!

Drugs—An Alternative Education

Presented at Youth Matters 1997—Dumfries Youth Festival Conference.

[*enter Graham and Barry in a car*]

G	Well, Barry
B	Graham. Got the gear?
G	Got the gear? Have I got the gear?
B	Yes the gear
G	What gear? [*Pause*] Ha! Ha! Wee joke there Barry ma man!
B	Don't do that! What have you got?
	[*Amelia enters—B and G freeze*]
Am	Loss of memory, bad skin, Can't remember the state I'm in, Popped a pill, Took a tab, Fought depression, fought the flab, Think it's trendy, think it's hard? No. [*Exit*]
G	I've got loads
B	Like what?
G	Algerian jellies, Magnolia MFI and some Middle East gear
B	Middle East?
G	Yeah—must be good eh? Eh? Middle East eh? That's . . .
B	Yes?
G	Well that's . . .
B	Yes?
G	Well it's . . . ehm the place
B	The place?
G	Yeah but it's **the** place—get me? **The** place
B	Yes **the** place and Middle East is **the** place
G	And it's Middle East gear
B	What is?
	[*Enter Jenny*]
J	Border controls and custom mazes,

The uses of mules and long drawn hazes,
Times I'm in dreams
Times I'm in . . .
Forgot made how what I'm saying,
Time has come down time that is slaying,
Time that is ending,
Time that is blending
In with each other
Till . . .

G The pills
B What pills?
G Look in the back [*B does*]
B Christ! It's Boots the Chemist.
[*G slams on the brakes*]
B What the . . . Jenny!
J Barry! [*G gets out of car*]
G Jenny! Listen fancy a good time?
J With either of you two? [*Both nod*] I'll phone you when I'm desperate
G Jenny, Jenny don't be so hasty!
B Wait till you see these!
J See what?
G Show her, show her. I'll watch for the fuzz
J Graham
G What?
J The only fuzz round here's in your belly button!
G Yeah? Very funny. But Barry and I have some serious gear likely to attract serious heat
J Why is it near the fire?
B No—it's in the car
J Where?
B The back seat. Come here
J Barry. You'll have to come up with something better than that
B What are you talking about?
J It'll take more than some rubbish about drugs to get me in the back seat with you!
B What! No. Just look
J Bring them out. [*Barry goes to do so*]
G Jen. These are serious Middle Eastern gear which you can't just bring . . .
B Here Jen [*Barry drops Smarties all over the floor*]
G Jeez Barry get these up off the floor. [*Jenny picks up one and looks at it carefully*]
J Where did you get these?
G Why? Got some better?
J I doubt it
G See Barry. Telt you it was good stuff
J My mother's angina tablets aren't this strong
G Angina tablets? Angina? These aren't angina tablets. These are Magnolia MFI

J They're what?
B Good gear Jen. That's what these are
G Fiver a bag
J Tell you what boys . . .
B What?
J I'll not pay anything but promise not to tell your mammies that you've raided the bathroom cabinet. [*Exit*]
G There goes someone who just doesn't know
B She does not does she?
G [*Picks up Smartie*] This will make us a fortune
B You reckon
G Yeah. [*Graham takes out a white pill and swallows it*]
B What's that?
G Eh? Oh some private stuff for me. Something special
B Give us one
G May as well—nothing's happening
B What at all?
G Nup
B How many've you had?
G About 15, 20
B Let me see one. [*Graham gives him one*]
G I got them off a bloke on the estate. Claims they're Eccie
B Graham, why's it got a big P on one side?
G I dunno
B Did they come in a bottle?
G Don't be daft. Poly bag. Sandwich bag
B Graham these are paracetamol
G Are they good gear?
B Graham come on. We've got an appointment with a nurse
G A nurse. See me . . . see birds, see me an birds. [*Exit*]
[*Enter Amelia*]
Am Fifteen. Up the duff.
[*Enter Jenny*]
J Eighteen. A widow
Am I'm away for my first French period in third year
J He's away for a pint of milk at
Am Nine in the morning. But I couldn't be bothered
J Going for it myself
Am So I met up with
J Him. The big man! Six foot of rank
Am Stupidity at my age. There were
J Six of them. Started knocking back the
Am Carry outs for everybody with
J Him. Next came the blow and he was
Am Stoned faces. He looked
J That stupid. Trying to walk along the wall

Am	Forty feet tall and Tom Cruise but
J	Falling forty feet after talking a
Am	Good game
J	Good game
Am	His place, ten seconds and a lifetime after
J	His gram, ten seconds and no lifetime hereafter. Still I hear some girl got made pregnant. One life comes as another goes. Symmetry according to the priest
Am	I heard some wife lost her husband. His life gone as another comes along. No children apparently. I wonder if she wants this one.
	[*Both get up*]
Am	It's more than the father does
J	Symmetry.
Am	One comes, one goes? No one cares
J	Both left.
Am and J	Thanks.

A Weekend Suicide Pact

This was written to be presented by young people as part of Dumfries Arts Festival in 1997. It can be adapted for whatever 'problem' by rewriting from *.

	[*Suzy enters on-stage and sits stage left. Dave enters a few moments after and sits S/R. They are in adjoining rooms. Suzy examines her face in an imaginery mirror facing the audience as Dave notices something out of his window. As Suzy does something, Dave reacts. When Suzy grimaces, Dave draws back etc.*]
Arlene	[*Off-stage*] Suzy! Suzy!
Suzy	What is it?
Arlene	Come here a minute!
Suzy	Why?
Arlene	Just come here!
Suzy	All right, all right. [*Exits*] What is it?
	[*After a pause enter Arlene*]
Arlene	I'm not staying
Suzy	It's only a bloody spider
Arlene	I don't care. It's the fifth spider since I went in to have my bath. And I still haven't had it
Dave	You can tell
Arlene	What did you say?
Suzy	Me? I never opened my mouth
Dave	Neither she did
Arlene	You did. [*Pause as she looks at her*] Do that again?
Suzy	Do what again?
Arlene	That! What you did
Dave	Oh you mean this?
Arlene	Yes!
Suzy	Have you been sampling the carry out?

Arlene	No!
Suzy	Listen! I'm away for a bath. You sit down there and don't drink anything till I get back
Arlene	I'll stand
Dave	You need to sit down
Arlene	I don't care I'll just stand
Suzy	OK . . . you . . . stand . . . then! [*Exits*]
Arlene	OK I will. [*Suzy leaves reluctantly*] OK. You can come out now
Dave	Come out of where?
Arlene	Wherever you're hiding
Dave	But I'm not hiding!
Arlene	Come off it!
Dave	I'm serious. I'm not hiding!
Arlene	Where are you then?
Dave	I'm around
Arlene	Who are you?
Dave	Are you sitting comfortably?
Arlene	Yes
Dave	Then I'll begin.
	[*Arlene starts reacting*]
Arlene	On you go
Dave	I'm an angel
Arlene	What?
Dave	I'm an angel
Arlene	I'm sure you are petal—now come out and we'll just phone the nice hospital and soon you'll be home amongst the nice doctors and nurses
Dave	You don't understand. I'm a real angel. [*Dave 'appears'*]
Arlene	How the . . .? Wait . . . How do you do that?
Dave	What? Appear? It's quite easy, well if you concentrate hard enough
Arlene	[*Sits down*] You are an angel aren't you?
Dave	Yup
Arlene	What are you doing here?
Dave	I'm here to see you
Arlene	You're what!
Dave	Look. The big man [*they both look up*] wants me to be an angel but I'm not too good at it so they've set me a test
Arlene	What kind of test?
Dave	I've got to save someone
Arlene	Who?
Dave	You
Arlene	Me?
Dave	Yes
Arlene	And if you don't?
Dave	It's the big bad fire.
	[*Arlene starts searching in her bag*]
Dave	What are you doing?

Arlene Looking for sun tan oil. You're going to need it where you're going

Dave [*Stops her*] Seriously Arlene. I've got 15 minutes to prove I can do it. [*Re-enter Suzy*]

Suzy AAAaaaagggghhhhhh!

Arlene What's the matter?

Suzy There's a bloody moth in there!

Arlene Christ!

Dave Who's she?

Arlene Suzy

Suzy What?

Dave A friend?

Arlene A friend

Suzy Thank you

Arlene Not you!

Suzy Not me?

Dave She's nice

Arlene She is

Suzy I am?

Dave She is!

Arlene Get your bloody eyes off!

Suzy Off what?

Arlene Off her

Suzy Off who?

Arlene Off you!

Suzy Off me?

Arlene Yes you!

Suzy Can I go home now?

Arlene Why?

Suzy This is obviously some care in the community scheme holiday I wasn't aware of. So if you don't mind I'll just leave you alone with your voices

Arlene Wait! Can she not see you?

Dave No. Nor hear me

Suzy Arlene. Take your hand off me. [*She does*] Now I'm wanting to spend the money [*Dave shakes his head*] getting pissed [*Dave shakes his head*] and thoroughly embarrassing myself [*Dave shrugs*] and you can do what the hell you like

Arlene Suzy! Get two glasses from the bathroom. I need a drink

Suzy There's a moth in the bathroom. You get the glasses. [*Exit Arlene*] [*Dave watches Suzy as she searches around the room looking for him. Suzy is looking under a chair when Arlene enters. Arlene stands for a second or two before speaking.*]

Arlene Suzy! [*Suzy bumps her head on the chair*] Glasses! [*Suzy gets up and pours*]

Arlene How did you get to come this weekend anyway

Dave This is no good. I want to know about you not her. I don't have time to save her too!

Suzy This is my study weekend. I'm supposed to be at Peter's aunt's
Arlene So she doesn't know that you're here
Suzy Of course she doesn't know. D'you think she'd let me come if she knew that we'd be here together without Peter's aunt's supervision?
Arlene What about Peter's aunt?
Suzy What about her?
Dave I hate to break up this wee party but . . .
Arlene Look would you just shut it!
Suzy Fine! If you don't want to listen
Arlene Not you!
Suzy Who then? Arlene this is getting right up my . . .
Arlene Look, will you just tell me why you lied
Suzy I needed away
Arlene Where's Peter now?
Suzy I don't know and I don't care
Arlene But he's little Peter's dad
Dave Look if I'd wanted an episode of Eastenders I would have paid my licence fee
Suzy Truth is I haven't seen little Peter since he was taken away by the adoption agency
Arlene But Suzy how could you let that kid be adopted?
Dave Christ, I give up
Arlene [*Quietly to Dave*] If you don't give it up soon it'll take Jesus himself to save you
Dave I've only got ten minutes left!
Arlene Then sit down, shut up and learn.

★

Suzy I was 16 when I got married to Peter. He was 17. I was five months pregnant waddling up the aisle. I wasn't the first to march to marriage carrying all before me. We were young and stupid, getting a job, buying our own furniture even. What did I get? Post-natal depression. Took me three years to learn how to spell it. But there it was. My condition. When Pete's mother suggested that little Peter was too much for me and that maybe at 16 it would be better to hand him over to a better life I nearly bit her hand off. I should have bit her tongue at the same time but when you're sitting day after day looking out of a window, rain dripping down making everything wet, watching all your pals giggling as they run for taxis in the pouring rain dressed for nights out in clothes you would kill for whilst your tracksuit bottoms don't quite reach your ankle you'd bloody well want to give the screaming child away. A nice home. A bath that wasn't stained. Clothes that didn't rip after three washings. Nappies that cost more than my weekly shopping. Peter couldn't cope. He looked at me, the pills I was popping and ran. Last I heard he was in a bedsit, occasionally selling *The Big Issue* in Perth or Dundee or somewhere. Little Peter is in a better place
Arlene How do you know?

SUZY I don't. But I can feel he's safe. Well looked after
ARLENE But how do you really know?
DAVE For God's sake! She knows!
ARLENE [*Scathingly*] For an angel you don't half swear a lot. No bloody wonder you've been sent down to save someone!
[*Suzy notices Arlene is 'talking to herself'*]
DAVE Well I'll be away a lot sooner if you'll let me save you!
ARLENE And from what exactly?
SUZY Arlene?
ARLENE Jesus!
SUZY Arlene? Are you OK?
ARLENE Eh? Yeah
SUZY Who are you talking to?
DAVE The name's Angel Pete
ARLENE Nobody. [*Looks at Dave*]
SUZY OK!
ARLENE Listen, where does Pete's aunt come into this?
SUZY She doesn't
ARLENE How?
SUZY She doesn't exist. I made her up. One day when I was really down I made her up so there was someone I could talk to. Every so often when I need to get away I'm, off to 85-year-old-bike-pushing Pete's Aunt for the weekend
ARLENE Has anyone never seen her then?
DAVE How the hell can anyone see her! She doesn't bloody exist!
ARLENE I wouldn't look into that too closely
SUZY Nobody does look into it closely. So nobody ever thinks to invite her over. That and the fact that she suffers from dementia, incontinence and scabies doesn't help her mobility
ARLENE I'd never get away with a lie like that
SUZY Uh huh?
ARLENE What?
SUZY And the cheque is in the post?
ARLENE Open your mouth
DAVE Sorry?
ARLENE It's . . . not for angel's ears
SUZY Arlene! And what whopper did we use this weekend?
ARLENE I'm studying for my finals
SUZY What are you going to do for graduation?
ARLENE You don't graduate when you fail
SUZY You can't fail. You've worked *so* hard
DAVE It doesn't say you're at college in your notes
SUZY How long have you been at college?
ARLENE Two years
DAVE You're not at college!
SUZY And nobody suspects?
ARLENE All my studying is done at the library. Train tickets to Glasgow produced

every so often. Pity I had no bursary granted and my parents had to support my study for two years

Dave Two years! You've been lying to your parents for two years?

Suzy What are you going to do?

Arlene I don't know. Do you know for two years she's hardly had a drink?

Suzy You've hardly been an angel

Dave At last!

Arlene I was four when I first realised. Tomato sauce bottle over my dad's head. Closely followed by the table. Plates, cutlery, the lot hit the fireplace. Hell of a fright? I was four. By ten I'd run out of excuses why we always had to play at other people's houses. I hid the bruises by wearing clothes. Do you know something? By the time I was old enough to make any sense of things I was starting to hear half-stories. About my brother, my mum and my dad—everybody

Suzy I didn't know you had a brother

Arlene I didn't know until I was eight

Suzy How?

Arlene One night they were both pissed. My mum decides to get out her box of momentoes. Throws the obituary from the local paper on my lap. I nearly wet myself. Eight-years old and I discover my brother died Nine years and three months previously. I felt *so* good

Suzy I would have killed her

Arlene I was eight. I waited my time. When I was thirteen she decided I needed my hair cut. I ran away. She caught me and dragged me by the hair all the way home

Suzy You're joking

Arlene No. So telling them I'm at college so that for two years they pay out to me rather than to Threshers or Oddbins isn't hard

Dave Is that it? I've been sent down here to save you by getting you to tell a couple of drunks . . .

Arlene Drunks? My parents aren't drunks. Got that? They're my mum and dad, that's who they are and don't you forget it!

Suzy Hey hey, settle down. [*Suzy gets up and knocks her bag over which rattles*]

Arlene What's in your bag? Suzy?

Suzy What?

Arlene Your bag. What's in your bag? [*Arlene takes bag*] Christ! Have you raided Boots?

Suzy [*Takes them off her*] They're working

Arlene Suzy. What are they there for? Why have you brought them with you?

Dave Be careful

Arlene Suzy. Why were you so desperate to come down here?

Dave She doesn't like people telling her what to do

Suzy I just needed to get away. Away from it all

Dave Calm her down

Arlene Stay calm Suzy

Suzy I'm fine. I'm OK. I just can't go back.

Dave	She can
Arlene	You can
Dave	She'll have people to care for her
Arlene	There are people who care for you
Suzy	Like who?
Dave	John
Arlene	John
Suzy	He doesn't like me
Dave	He does
Arlene	He does
Dave	He sent the Valentine
Arlene	He sent you that Valentine?
Suzy	How did you know about that?
Dave	He told you
Arlene	He told me
Suzy	You know him?
Dave	You met on the train to Glasgow
Arlene	He meets me on the train to Glasgow
Suzy	He said he liked me?
Dave	He likes your beautiful blue eyes, your cheeks when you smile and the way you laugh
Arlene	He said he liked you
Dave	Suzy I'm so sorry
Arlene	I'm sorry Suzy
Suzy	What for?
Arlene	[*To Dave*] What for?
Dave	She has to get rid of the pills
Arlene	The pills!
Suzy	You're sorry for the pills?
Dave	Don't let on you know
Arlene	For thinking that you were going to do yourself in
Suzy	Oh right. Well I wasn't right
Arlene	Yes
Suzy	So I think they're dangerous don't you?
Dave	There's children downstairs
Arlene	Did you see the kids downstairs?
Suzy	God yeah! I wouldn't want to have them getting hold of them
Arlene	No! Why don't you let me flush them down the toilet?
Suzy	Yeah [*goes into bag*] Christ I forgot I had this [*picks up photograph*]
Arlene	What is it?
Suzy	A photograph of Peter. Here. [*Hands it to Arlene who looks horrified*] What's the matter with you? You look as if you've seen a ghost!
Arlene	No, just an angel
Suzy	Peter was no angel! [*Exits*]
Dave	[*Looks at picture*] Apparently so. Listen, one day I'll be able to see her or talk to her. Until then . . . never mind. Bye

Arlene	Hey wait a minute! You were supposed to save me!
Dave	Apparently some guy called Gabriel has suggested that you'll only be saved by the second coming
Arlene	Gee ta!
Dave	You're welcome. [*Exit*]
	[*Re-enter Suzy*]
Suzy	Is he away then?
Arlene	Who?
Suzy	Whoever you've been talking to in your head! Do you know I'm worried about you?
Arlene	So am I
Suzy	Why?
Arlene	The pubs have been open for four hours and I'm still sober! [*Exit*]

The following were all presented at a parents' conference. The conference was the first time the Director of Education's daughter had performed with us. Her father was in the audience and did applaud!

Boyfriends

Suzy	Who you waiting on?
Laura	My boyfriend!
Suzy	You're too young to have a boyfriend
Laura	I am not
Suzy	Yes you are
Laura	I'm not, not, not!
Suzy	What age are you then?
Laura	I'm sixteen
Suzy	No!
Laura	Am so!
Suzy	What age is your boyfriend then?
Laura	27
Suzy	[*Bursts out laughing*] Never!
Laura	He is . . . nearly. He's 17
Suzy	[*Pause*] Are you?
Laura	Am I what?
Suzy	Are you? You know! Are you?
Laura	What? Going to hockey tonight?
Suzy	No!
Laura	What then?
Suzy	I mean are you doing it? With him?
Laura	Doing what with who?
Suzy	Are you doing sex with your boyfriend?
Laura	[*Long pause while she looks 'angry' at Suzy*] Do I look the kind of woman that 'does' sex with my boyfriend?

Suzy I don't know
Laura What do you mean you don't know?
Suzy You tell me what someone who does sex with her boyfriend looks like and I'll tell you if you look the same
Laura You know what I mean. [*Stares at Suzy*]
Suzy [*Pause*] No!
Laura Thank Christ for that—if my father ever thought I was doing it he'd kill me. I mean what with Aids and teenage pregnancy and the risk of STD it just isn't safe being 16 anymore
Suzy I know what you mean. My dad still thinks I haven't started my periods
Laura No!
Suzy Straight up! I'm telling you. He once burst in on me when I was in the shower right—well I was out the shower with a towel on, but his face would have lit up the High Street because I was shaving my legs!
Laura Parents eh?
Suzy Yeah. What time's he due?
Laura Half an hour ago
Suzy Stood up?
Laura No. Half an hour's good going for him. Usually it's an hour
Suzy What age is your dad?
Laura 50. Why?
Suzy So's my dad
Laura So?
Suzy Well this is nearly the 90s and our fathers are both 50. So they would have been 20 in the the Sixties!
Laura Woodstock
Suzy Drugs
Laura Rock
Suzy Roll
Laura Free love!
BOTH [*Horrified*] My parents! Yeuch!
[*Exit*]

Desparate Drugs

Ryan What you got?
Diane £20
Ryan Enough for a half dig
Diane Between two?
Ryan I've got tabs. We'll be all right.
[*Enter older boy*]
Darren All right Ryan?
Ryan Eh? Yeah! Here. [*Gives money to Darren*]
Darren Gee ta!
Diane Where's our stuff?
Darren Where's my money?

Diane He just gave you £20
Darren Did he?
Ryan Come on Darren. Next week I'll pay you it all back
Diane Pay what back? What are you talking about?
Ryan Nothing Diane now shut it
Diane Ryan. What are you on?
Darren Ryan? Everything?
Ryan Well no. Don't give me it Diane, you've got to believe me. I'm not
Darren You're not what Ryan?
Diane Ryan?
Ryan Ryan Armaan, aged 15. Caught in possession, head still reeling
Diane Diane Smith, Ryan's pal. Stood in the corner, no help when he fell
Darren Darren No Second Name
Don't try. I won't take the blame.
Ryan was 12 when he began.
It wasn't forced to comfort he ran
Ryan Care panel, care panel
Diane Did you know that 85 per cent of young people are in care due to no fault of their own?
Ryan Care panel, care panel
Diane Did you know that we still think social work a dirty term
Ryan Broken hearts, broken bodies
Darren Thanks for the prejudice!
You know you helped me do it.
The only ones to screw it up was you!
Ryan Broken ribs; broken nose. [*Ryan slumps on the floor*]
Diane Ryan! Ryan! Can you hear me Ryan?
[*Enter two girls*]
Darren Girls. Fancy some excitement?
Jessica What? Like him?
Darren He was from a broken childhood of dreams. You girls look mature enough to 'handle'
Tracy Handle?
Darren This. [*Takes out packet*]
[*Exit girls and Darren*]
Diane [*Left, with Ryan*] Ryan! Get up Ryan!

Bully for You

Two young people are seen loitering, talking about 'her' and when she's likely to turn up

A What's the time
B Ten to
A She's late
B Yep
A So eh what will we do?

B Wait
A Why?
B It's worth it. Look here she comes.
[*Enter C*]
A Hide.
[*B enters the crowd*]
C Christ!
A Where you going?
C Nowhere
A [*Corners her against the wall. puts hands on her cheek*] Where's nowhere?
C Look, you going to leave me alone?
A Why? You scared?
C No.
[*B re-enters*]
B Yeah, she is
C What the . . .
[*B Grabs her wrists and forces her against the wall*]
A Give us it
C [*Looks anxiously at one and then the other*] What?
A [*Strokes her cheek again*] You see. We know what you're like
B Yeah, we got told.
A So hurry up!
[*B lets her wrists go*]
C [*Takes out £10*] Here. [*She gives it to A*]
B What about me?
C [*Takes out £1 coin*] Here
B What's this?
C It's all I've got.
[*A starts laughing*]
B [*Takes knife to A's throat*] Your turn.
[*A stops laughing and hands over £10 note and backs next to C. They cower together*]
B Just consider it a successful take-over bid.
[*A and C disappear*]
B [*Turns to audience*] What are you lot looking at?
[*Exit*]

Creating Smoke

A Would you look at the state of that!
B What? What?
A That!
B Yeah but where?
A That one there, look her
B Her!
A The one on the left
B Yeah.

[*A thumps him one*]
B What did you do that for?
A That's my mum
B Aww
A What are you doing?
B What do you mean?
A What are you doing? [*No response*] Here! [*No response*] Now!
B [*Pause*] Talking to you
A Yeah. But why?
B Any fags?
A Fags?
B Yeah
A Nup
B How not?
A I don't smoke
B I do
A Yeah
B But I haven' t got any
A So?
B Do you have any?
A Brian, I don't smoke and I don't have any fags
B [*Pause*] But I need one
A Why?
B What do you mean?
A Why do you smoke?
B Why does anybody smoke?
A Beats me
B I'll tell you then
A I didn't mean I didn't . . .
B You see it is an inalienable right for humans beings, unlike animals, because we have thumb and animals don't have thumbs, to do what we want
A But why do you smoke?
B Andy
A Yes
B Ask your mum. She smokes doesn't she?
A Yeah so?
B Why does she smoke?
A Because as a young person, through advertising, she got sucked into believing that it was the right thing to do. Film, television, all commercial media supported and promoted the cigarette as a social tool. [*There is a pause—A looks at audience*]
B But advertising cigarettes on the TV's banned
A Quite right
B And you hardly ever see any actors in any programmes lighting up
A And?
B So why does your mum smoke?

A She can't help it!
B Then neither can I
A But you're young, you've your whole life ahead
B Hey wait a minute!
A What?
B I've got it!
A OK, why do you smoke?
B Just because. Just cos I want to! Look!! [*Produces bent cigarette*] I've found one!
A Are you going to put that in your mouth?
B Eh? Yeah! [*Does so*] Andy?
A What?
B Got a light?
[*A exits*]
B Andy!

Fablespake

A few years ago I found some rather wonderful Scottish tales. I fashioned them into workshop cliffhangers, where they work very well, and a short play entitled *Fablespake*. The workshops all have 'endings' which I normally profferred to the group after they improvised their own. You can use them as one act plays, or as a collection.

You may be able to find other local stories that will work just as well.

My own self

Fiona is a wee girl who will just not go to bed. Her mother finally despairs of her and tells her that she herself is away to bed. Before she goes however she warns Fiona about the Fire Spirit who will come and take her away if she's not too careful. Fiona thinks her mother is talking nonsense until a small sprite falls out of the fire onto the hearth.

Fiona is asked her name and replies that she's 'just her own self'. The sprite is surprised for that is who she is too. They begin playing together until Fiona drops a spark that harms the Fire Spirit. The Fire Spirit demands to know who is playing in the hearth. The sprite replies 'just my own self'. 'With whom are you playing' demands the Spirit. 'Oh just my own self too' replies the spirit. What happened next?

The legend's ending

The legend states that the sprite's answer saved Fiona, for the very next minute a gigantic hand swept down and took the spirit back into the fire.

The house of Inverawe

The Laird in a Highland castle enjoys both privilege and responsibility. When a man runs into your castle and demands protection, as he is being chased by two men trying to kill him in revenge, your responsibility is to listen and judge if your privilege is to be extended to his protection.

As he tells you that he killed a man in a fair fight and you believe that he speaks the truth, you take him to be someone worthy of your protection. You offer him bed and board for the night. When two of your kinsmen rush in some time later to tell you that they have been chasing a man who killed your half brother, you realise your mistake. But the rules of Laird's hospitality and the fact that you gave your word stops you from giving the man up.

From that point onwards the ghost of your brother comes to see you three nights running to deliver a warning. Now what warning would that be and did it come true?

The legend's ending

The ghost told the Laird at the last visitation that they would meet up again at Triconderoga. The Laird knew of no such place and ordered his people to search all the maps. No one found it anywhere.

Many years later the Laird was a Scottish soldier fighting the French in America.

He talked to one of the Indian guides who told him all about the fort that he was about to attack. Fort Carillion was supposed to be easy to take. However the night before he called his officers together and told them that the following day they would have to finish the fighting themselves. Everyone thought he was off his head until the very next day a stray bullet caught him in the chest. His last words were 'Triconderoga peace at last!'. Fort Carillion was known locally to the Indians as Triconderoga.

The Laird of Co

There once was a Laird who was well thought of and well respected. The locals saw him as the person to go to in time of need. One small boy came running up to him when he was out a walk and asked for some ale for the pan he was carrying. His mother was sick and the physician thought that it would do her some good.

The Laird agreed and sent him over to the big house to ask at the kitchen for his ale. When the boy arrived the butler didn't believe his story and gave him a really hard time. When the butler was given the pan he took it away to fill up.

The first barrel emptied and the butler had hardly filled up the pan at all. The butler shoved the pan back at the boy but the boy only shook his head and gave him it back. The second barrel filled it up very quickly and the butler was happy to get rid of a bogle from his kitchen.

Some years passed before the boy was able to pay the Laird back. How did he do it?

The legend's ending

Some time passed and the Laird found himself in a foreign jail as a prisoner of war. Condemned to death he began dreaming of times passed and of the hills and the house that he had left way behind. He thought of the small boy that he had helped and wondered what had become of him. He started to imagine that he could see him until he found that he could hear him. The small boy was standing right before him whilst all the guards were asleep. The wee boy said,

'Laird of Co., rise and go! If ye be free, follow me!'

The Laird followed through gates that had been locked and past the snoring guards. The boy turned to leave with the words, 'one good turn deserves another: I to you, you to my mother.'

The Master of Orrick

The master was a wizard of whom all were frightened. When his father heard that Jamie wanted to serve his apprenticeship there before becoming a wizard himself he tried all in his power to persuade him not to go.

Jamie was a head strong lad who would not be turned and off he went to serve for the next few years. The master greeted him at the door as if he were expecting him. Jamie overcame his initial fear and listened with all the others in the Great Hall to the rules: in bed by nine, attending all the classes, no misbehaviour, little time to yourself and then the last day. On the last day all of the apprentices would line up to leave and the last one to leave would stay forever with the master.

Jamie started patchily turning some of his classmates green instead of into frogs and kept making the wrong mixture from the wrong ingredients and so on. Eventually he became the best in the class and then came the last day . . .

The legend's ending

On the very last day Jamie lined up with the rest. When the master rang the bell for them to leave all of the class except Jamie ran for the door. The master walked behind him and stopped him before he walked out of the door.

'I had hoped it would be you Jamie,' said the master. Jamie was unimpressed and pointed at his shadow behind him. 'Oh but master there is still one behind me.'

From that day onward there began the story of a great wizard, the Master of Orrick who did great things for all folk but didn't have a shadow.

The ghost of Meggarine Castle

There were two young travellers who had come upon a castle where they were to stay the night. One had stayed before but for the other it was the first time. They had rooms next to one another, or so they thought.

One was there to find out if it was true about the ghost that walked the castle at night. The second traveller was not as keen as the first to find out about this ghost!

During the night they both heard faint but persistent knocking. They both thought that it was coming from the other's room. Both at the same time ran out of their room to find the other in the corridor and then discovered . . .

The legend's ending

They found out from the maid the next morning that the knocking came from a haunted room between them. The Clan Menzies had owned the castle once and the wife of one of the chief's had made him very angry for some reason.

The chief was slightly mad and killed her. He told the Community around him that she had . . .

Een ghost of Huntly

Seven miles west of Dundee, there's an old house built in the fifteenth century. It was owned by the Lyon family of Glamis. One of their daughters fell in love with a manservant. The chief thought this ridiculous and banned her from ever seeing him again.

The chief thought of a way to keep her from the manservant. However she managed to break free with tragic circumstances . . .

The legend's ending

She was heart broken and when put in the high tower vowed to break out. She managed to get out one windy night by throwing herself to her death.

THE EPILOGUE

Conclusion

Now that you've read the book, or browsed and picked out what you want to use—what next? Well, when I started all this, all I wanted was to introduce an idea—that drama can be used easily and without fear in youth work. If I've succeeded in convincing you to try, then great—it was money well spent.

This is, however, a fairly stylised book and I have written about what worked for me and quite a few others. Now you've finished with this you can skip into the bibliography and progress. There are more advanced and more specialised books for you to go after. However you may want to use them like I suggested you use this book—when and where it works. Then you can create your own methodology and your own bank of ideas. If we can put drama into the mainstream of youth work then I believe that we will be able to produce more dynamic and youth empowered youth work. As I began by saying in my introduction—this can knock the Director of Education's 15 minute diatribe into a cocked hat. Now how many of us wish that to happen!

Useful Contacts

The theatre is full of representative organisations who have a plethora of interesting material and resources that are well worth getting your hands on. In this age of electronic wizardry some of them have web sites and on screen order forms.

Organisations

From amateur drama to youth theatre to unions there are a wide number of representative organisations. They have a wide range of resources and helpful hints. They should also be able to offer advice if you have a particularly interested young person. Where possible I have noted the Scottish/Welsh/Irish associations and headquarters. Call the English HQ for advice or to complain about the lack of a nationally impressive spread.

Association of Professional Theatre for Children and Young People
Unicorn Arts Theatre
6/7 Great Newport Street
London WC2H 7JB
Tel: 0171 836 3623
Fax: 0171 8365366
APT aims to promote and develop the work of professional theatre organisations and individuals working for or with children and young people.

Drama Association of Wales
The Library
Singleton Road
Splott
Cardiff CF2 2ET
Tel: 01222 452200
Fax: 01222 452277
At the heart of the Drama Association of Wales member services is the largest specialist drama lending library in the world! There are over 100,000 volumes of plays, biographies, critical works and technical theatre books in the DAW library which includes the entire playsets and lending collections of the former British Theatre Association. DAW offers a tremendous range of services to community drama, script and drape hire, an extensive training programme, new writing and youth theatre.

National Association of Youth Theatres
Unit 1304
The Custard Factory
Gibb Street
Digbeth
Birmingham B9 4AA
Tel: 0121 608 2111
Fax: 0121 608 2333

National Youth Music Theatre
5th Floor
The Place Theatre
Shaftesbury Avenue
London W1V 8AY
Tel: 0171 734 7478
Fax: 0171 734 7515

National Youth Theatre of Great Britain
443–445 Holloway Road
London N7 6LW
Tel: 0171 281 3863
Fax: 0171 281 8246

Scottish Youth Theatre
Gordon Chambers
90 Mitchell Street
Glasgow G1 3NQ
Tel: 0141 221 5127
Fax: 0141 221 9123
E-mail: sy100@post.almac.co.uk

British Actors Equity Association
Guild House
Upper St Martin's Lane
London WC2H 9EG
Tel: 0171 379 6000
Fax: 0171 379 7001

Scottish Office:
65 Bath Street
Glasgow G2 2BX
Tel: 0141 332 1669

Northern Office:
Conavon Court
12 Blackfriars Street
Salford M3 5BQ
Tel: 0161 832 3183

Welsh Office:
Transport House
1 Cathedral Road
Cardiff CF1 9SD
Tel: 01222 397971

BECTU – Broadcasting Entertainment Cinematograph & Theatre Union
111 Wardour Street
London W1V 4AY
Tel: 0171 437 8506
Fax: 0171 437 8268

The Arts Council of England
14 Great Peter Street
London SW1P 3NQ
Tel: 0171 333 0100

Arts Council of Wales
Holst House
9 Museum Place
Cardiff CF1 3NX
Tel: 01222 394711
Fax: 01222 221447

Arts Council of Northern Ireland
185 Stranmills Road
Belfast BT9 5DU
Tel: 01232 381591
Fax: 01232 661715

The Scottish Arts Council
12 Manor Place
Edinburgh EH3 7DD
Tel: 0131 226 6051
Fax: 0131 225 9833

The London Academy of Music & Dramatic Art
Tower House
226 Cromwell Road
London SW5 0SR
Tel: 0171 373 9883
Fax: 0171 370 4739

Birmingham School of Speech & Drama
45 Church Road
Edgbaston
Birmingham B15 3SW
Tel: 0121 454 3424
Fax: 0121 456 4996

Bristol Old Vic Theatre School
2 Downside Road
Clifton
Bristol BS8 2XF
Tel: 0117 973 3535
Fax: 0117 923 9371

Rose Bruford College
Lamorbey Park
Sidcup
Kent DA15 9DF
Tel: 0181 300 3024
Fax: 0181 308 0542

The Central School of Speech & Drama
The Embassy Theatre
64 Eton Avenue
Swiss Cottage
London NW3 3HY
Tel: 0171 722 8183
Fax: 0171 722 4132

The Arts Educational London Schools
Cone Ripman House
14 Bath Road
Chiswick
London W4 1LY
Tel: 0181 994 9366
Fax: 0181 994 9274

Cygnet Training Theatre
New Theatre
Friars Gate
Exeter EX2 4AZ
Tel: 01392 77189

Drama Centre London
176 Prince of Wales Road
London NW5 3PT
Tel: 0171 267 1177

East 15 Acting School
Hatfields
Rectory Lane
Loughton
Essex IG10 3RU
Tel: 0181 508 5983

Guildford School of Acting
Millmead Terrace
Guildford
Surrey GU2 5AT
Tel: 01483 560701
Fax: 01482 35431

Guildhall School of Music & Drama
Barbican
London EC2V 8DT
Tel: 0171 628 2571
Fax: 0171 256 9438

Mountview Theatre School
104 Crouch Hill
London N8 9EA
Tel: 0181 340 5885
Fax: 0181 348 1727

Manchester Metropolitan University
Capitol Building
School Lane
Didsbury
Manchester M20 0HT
Tel: 0161 247 2000 Ext. 7123

Weber Douglas Academy of Dramatic Art
30 Clareville Street
London SW7 5AP
Tel: 0171 370 4154
Fax: 0171 373 5639

Royal Academy of Music & Drama
62–64 Gower Street
London WC1E 6ED
Tel: 0171 636 7076
Fax: 0171 323 3865

Royal Scottish Academy of Music & Drama
100 Renfrew Street
Glasgow G2 3DB
Tel: 0141 332 4101
Fax: 0141 332 8901

Welsh College of Music & Drama
Castle Grounds
Cathays Park
Cardiff CF1 3ER
Tel: 01222 342854
Fax: 01222 237639

The Internet

As explained earlier there are now a number of internet sites for youth orientated theatre. I have included a sample. This is by no means exhaustive and would suggest you 'surf' and explore.

School Show Page [http://www.schoolshows.demon.co.uk]
This is an excellent site and well worth the visit. It currently includes (as at end 1998):

- Reviews of stage plays.
- Notes on directing a show; improvisation; working on drama within a school; working with boys; texts; rehearsals; creating a company and money for the show.

As a comparative guide to this book it is very helpful.

UK Theatre Web [http://www/uktw.co.uk]
Can be used as an access point or link page to other theatre pages. It is in sections so that you can choose directly where you want to go to.

Amdram Heaven [http://www/amdram.or.uk]
As with most things done by people with a love or passion this is cared for regularly. There are many sections and links to other sites.

The Childrens' Theatre Pages [http://www/members.ao/com/theatreuk/main.htm]
This is another 'entry' site with links to many other sites worth visiting. The contents of the site include some resources and comments. Worth visiting to get into the professional sites like Polka's, the National Association of Youth Theatres etc.

Stage Kids [http://www.stagekids.com]
One of the American based sites which includes kits for performances, iand perhaps surprisingly, issues such as substance abuse and environmental awareness.

Samuel French [http://www.samuelfrench-london.co.uk]
Perhaps the largest handler of performance rights and scripts in the UK. The web site is very informative but for more than the basic information I would use more conventional methods. The addresses and phone/fax numbers follow on from these.

Bibliography

I have not read all of these books. Had I done so my PhD would be amongst them! I have listed them in no particular order and without any commentary other than *their* own. Pick those that appeal, refuse to entertain those that don't and don't blame your Visa bill on me! I'm sure that there are some that repeat the lessons of others!

Bailey, Sally Dorothy. *Wings to Fly*. Bringing Theatre Arts to Students with Special Needs. In this rare resource teachers will find all the information they require to teach theatre arts to students with disabilities. In addition, the author describes ways to use drama as a tool to teach traditional subjects, such as science and social studies.

Banks, R. A. *Drama and Theatre Arts*. Primarily intended for those studying drama and theatre arts for examinations such as GCSE and A levels, but it is also of great interest to the general reader, those studying drama at college, and those interested in amateur dramatics.

Barker, Clive. *Theatre Games. A New Approach to Drama Training*. The games in this handbook are all designed to enable anyone interested in acting to develop their technique without inhibition or artificiality. The games are arranged in order of complexity from a simple game of tag to much more complex games. A very suitable book for anyone involved in performance or teaching.

Berry, Mary and Clamp, Michael. *Drama Through the Ages*. This book is to inspire lower secondary school students to explore literature through active and varied approaches. It is divided into thematic sections with illustrations to help place the writings in context. The suggested activities and notes are for group work and individual study.

Birch, David. *The Language of Drama*. This book is about the critical strategies that can be used to understand the dynamic processes involved in writing, reading, analying, rehearsal, producing and reception of drama in both the classroom and the professional theatre.

Boagey, Eric. *Starting Drama*. This is a book for the year preceding GCSE, when the students are starting their preliminary work for the drama examination. Two 'presenters' show how drama developed and introduce the actors, dramatists and audiences of their times. Their dialogues are followed by ideas to stimulate dramatic imagination and its practical expression.

Bolton, Gavin. *Acting in Classroom Drama. A Critical Analysis*. Foreword by David Davis. Classroom drama is now a widespread component of primary and secondary school curricula, both in its own right and as a support for other subjects. Whilst there are many exponents and practitioners, there is a lack of overall analysis of theory, advocating practice and evaluation. This analysis is now available in this objective and penetrating book.

Bolton, Gavin. *New Perspective on Classroom Drama*. An alternative guide for both the specialist and non-specialist drama teacher. It puts the spotlight primarily on classroom drama, although it also offers advice on the basic understanding pupils need to approach the production of a school play.

Booth, David. *Story Drama. Reading, Writing and Roleplaying Across a Curriculum.* David Booth argues that roleplay is a natural way in which young people can explore the world around them and suggests classroom models and simple frameworks for creating a safe, interactive, enriching environment.

Bower, Jane. *Ways Into Drama. Storylines, Activities and Visual Aids for Starting Lessons. A Guide for the Primary Teacher.* This handbook contains ten storylines with cross-curricular possibilities. It also offers a selection of practical and visual ways into drama sessions.

Boyd, Neva L. *Handbook of Recreational Games.* This book contains the rules for many common games that children play, often without knowing the full extent of the game, and instructions for many other games they probably have never heard of. Eighteen categories of games are covered with up to 59 games (plus variations) in a category.

Clipson-Boyles, Suzi. *Drama in Primary English Teaching.* This book aims to provide primary teachers with drama opportunities for their pupils as required by the National Curriculum Order for English, and includes activities relating to the range of fiction and non-fiction outlined in the National Literacy Framework.

Brandes, Donna and Phillips, Howard. *Gamesters' Handbook. 140 Games for Teachers and Group Leaders.* This book has been welcomed by teachers and group leaders running every kind of group session. It is an invaluable collection, offering 140 different activities, exercises and strategies, which the authors have tried and tested through years of teaching experience.

Brandes, Donna and Norris, John. *The Gamesters' Handbook 3.* A collection of valuable games for developing self-awareness, confidence, assertiveness, decision-making skills, trust, and also just for fun.

Bray, Errol. *Playbuilding. A Guide for Group Creation of Plays with Young People.* A guide for teachers, youth theatre workers and youth leaders, for group creation of plays with young people. It offers detailed instructions on creating plays using one word or brief phrase lead-ins.

Butterfield, Tony in association with Atonia Sieveking. *Drama Through Language Through Drama.* A highly successful method which streses the point that both students and teachers are actors. Emphasis is placed not only on the verbal but also on the non-verbal expression promoting active rather than passive learning.

Mc Caslin, Nellie. *Creative Drama in the Intermediate Grades.* This book is designed so that the teacher with no experience can immediately begin teaching creative drama in the intermediate grades. It contains all the methodology, all the content, all the lesson components necessary to teach several sequences of creative drama in the three intermediate grades.

Mc Caslin, Nellie. *Creative Drama in the Primary Grades.* This book contains two courses of instruction—a methodology for teachers and curriculum material for students. Based on the theory that one learns best by doing, the book is designed so that the teacher with no experience can immediatley begin teaching creative drama in the elementary grades.

Cassady, Marsh. *Great Scenes from Minority Playwrights.* Seventy-four scenes of cultural diversity.

Cassady, Marsh. *The Theatre and You. A Beginning.* Deals with five main subject areas: getting aquainted with theatre; directing; design; acting; and a history of the theatre.

Cattanach, Ann. *Drama for People with Special Needs*. Drama can be used as a means of helping and healing those people who have special needs. The book concentrates on the practical methods of dramatical exploration which can be shared with groups or individuals. Dramatherapy can be used with adults or children, individuals or groups.

Chambers, Aidan. *Plays for Young People to Read and Perform*. In this critical bookguide, Aidan Chambers sketches the historical background to plays written for and performed by children and young people. And in discussions of more than eighty plays and collections of one-act dramas he places children's theatrical literature in the context of children's literature as a whole, a study here undertaken for the first time.

Clifford, Sara and Herrmann, Anna. *Making a Leap. Theatre of Empowerment. A Practical Handbook for Creative Drama Work with Young People*. Foreword by Alec Davison. Suitable for use by both experienced theatre practitioners and beginners, the book provides a model that is adaptable for work with diverse groups of young people over different timescales—a day, a week, or a period of months.

Cooper, Simon and Mackey, Sally. *Theatre Studies. An Approach for Advanced Level*. This is a clear, comprehensive and long-awaited textbook for students of A-Level courses in theatre studies and drama. This unique and vital resource addresses the four major sections of the written papers by offering: textual analysis for set texts with commentary and analysis; frameworks for set text study; reviews and analysis of contemporary productions; background information on key practitioners—Artaud, Brecht, Craig and Stanislavski.

Courtney, Richard. *Play, Drama and Thought. The Intellectual Background to Dramatic Education*. This important reference work is essential reading for drama educators, therapists, and others in the helping profession. The book looks at drama from a philosopical perspective, the psychology of drama, the author considers drama from a broader sociological and anthropological view giving us a glimpse of its importance in cultures distant from each other in time and space. It also shows how drama relates to intuition, symbolism, and the fundamental structure of human thought.

Davies, Gaynor. *The Primary Performance Handbook*. A practical, effective and easy-to-use guide for teachers who want to explore the presentation of drama in the primary school in more depth. Its rationale is a balance of practical activity and intellectual discipline.

Davies, Geoff. *Practical Primary Drama*. Designed for teachers with little or no experience, this book has many useful suggestions on how to prepare and conduct drama sessions, the difficulty of doing drama in a hall or classroom and ideas for lessons are discussed.

Davison, Alec and Gordon, Peter. *Games and Simulations in Action*. HB. This practical handbook for teachers, youth leaders, group organizers and lecturers explores how to use role-play, gaming and simulation as a central and everyday means of active learning in all subjects and at all levels.

Deary, Terence. *Teaching Through Theatre*. Six Practical Projects. The plays in this book began as ideas, which were developed by actors through discussion, improvisation and finally practical experiments involving children. These projects are suitable for performance by schools, adult amateur and professional groups.

Dennis, Anne. *The Articulate Body. The Physical Training of the Actor*. This book considers the unique responsibility of the actor to convey, through his physical being, the thoughts and feelings of the theatrical event.

Dowling, Clare and Williams, Caroline. *Class Acts. Monologues for Teenagers.* With an introduction by Dermot Bolger. Thirty lively, contemporary monologues for use in the classroom or drama workshop. Diverse range of themes including bullying, holiday romances, exam pressure, career choices and relationships. An invaluable aid for teachers and students alike.

Dowling, Kevin. *Brodies' Notes English Coursework Poetry and Drama.* Focused on all areas of investigation that will help English Literature and their teachers. By using the thematic approach, they aim to stimulate imaginative involvement with a selection of feats which share some comparability of theme, genre or intention.

Engelsman, Alan and Penny. *Theatre Arts. An Introductory Course. Student Handbook.* Young thespians will delight in this updated version of the Theatre Arts I Student Handbook. This text offers secondary students the opportunity to expand their theatre knowledge and experience through improvising and playing theatre games.

Engelsman, Alan and Penny. *Theatre Arts I. An Introductory Course. Teacher's Course Guide.* Teachers of high school and middle school drama will enjoy using this updated version of the guide. This innovative text stresses the importance of both improvisation and theatre games in the artistic development of young thespians.

England, Alan. *Theatre for the Young.* The book focuses on theatre provided for the young by adult professionals and amateurs. It considers the claim of such theatre to be regarded as an important cultural phenomenom in its own right, and examines the various debates that arise from the development of children's theatre.

Evans, C. and Smith, L. *Acting and Theatre.* Every aspect of the theatrical world is covered in this exciting introduction to acting and theatre. It illustrates and explains some of the ways actors train and rehearse, as well as going into the practical arts of set props and costume design and the technical basics of theatre lighting and sound.

Fleaming, Michael. *Starting Drama Teaching.* This book is about the theory and more especially the practice of drama teaching in primary and secondary schools. It is aimed primarily at teachers who are new to drama, but will also appeal to those with more experience but who wish to update and broaden their range.

Fleming, Michael. *The Art of Drama Teaching.* This book provides a multitude of practical ideas for teachers, student teachers, and those who are interested in using drama to teach other subjects. It is practical in orientation but has a significant theoretical dimension.

Foster, John L. *Drama.* Books 1 and 3. This series offers all the resources you need to create a basic English course for the lower years of secondary school. The range of material is rich and varied drawing on verse, story, drama and language material from many cultures and many contexts.

Foster, John L. *Drama 3. Basic English Series.* A basic course for the lower years of secondary schools consisting of five short plays by various authors, accompanied by practical exercises under the headings: activities, presenting the play, thinking about the characters, thinking about the situations and writing your own script.

Graham, Ginny. *First Stage. A Drama Handbook for Schools and Youth Theatres.* This invaluable handbook offers a wide range of creative ideas and practical advice to all those working with young people on the organisation and content of drama sessions, as well as the performance of both scripted and devised plays.

Harrison, Larraine S. *Learning Through Play. Dance and Drama.* This series contains a wealth of new pratical structured play activities for three to five year olds. All the activities are based on the areas of learning for under-fives recommended by the School Curriculum and Assessment Authority.

Hayes, Jennifer and Schinder, Dorothy. *Pioneer Journeys: Drama in Museum Education.* Explains techniques using drama to help us understand artwork and become invovled with it.

Heald, Chris. *Role Play and Drama. Bright Ideas for Early Years.* Role play and drama provide young children with one of the best environment in which to learn. This book outlines the importance of role play and drama in the early years classroom and provides a wide range of practical activities, in both real and imaginary contexts, to enable children to explore their world. The ideas and activities are easy to follow and clearly illustrated.

Heathcote, Dorothy and Bolton, Gavin. *Drama for Learning. Dorothy Heathcote's Mantle of the Expert Approach to Education.* Drama for Learning pushes the boundaries of learning, using drama as an impetus for productive learning across the curriculum, from language arts to history, maths and science.

Heing, Ruth Beall. *Creative Drama for the Classroom Teacher.* Designed for teachers of elementary school children, this volume presents a collection of practical, progressive techniques for learning and teaching creative drama.

Hornbrook, David. *Education in Drama.* 'At last a text which unites drama and cultural diversity within a critical art/education framework. In yet another thought-provoking book, David Hornbrook argues persuasively for a culturally balanced arts curriculum.' Maggie Semple, Education Planning Officer, Arts Council of Great Britain.

Jackson, Tony (Ed.). *Learning Through Theatre.* New Perspectives on Theatre in Education. Aiming to stimulate and inform, it will be of practical interest to teachers, educationalists, theatre practitioners and students of drama and education alike.

James, Ronald. *Drama Developing.* A collection of scripted drama lessons, with phrased stories intended to be read out by a teacher in order to provoke younger pupils' own interpretation of the stories and for them to act it out as the story develops.

Jennings, Sue. *Dramatherapy. Theory and Practice 2.* HB. Provides both clinician and theatre artist with a stimulating overview of the most recent developments in the field. The international contributors, all practising dramatherapists or psychotherapists, offer a wide variety of perspectives from contrasting theoretical backgrounds, showing them how it is possible to integrate a dramatherapeutic approach into many different ways of working toward mental health.

Jennings, Sue. *Dramatherapy with Families Groups and Individuals. Waiting in the Wings.* HB. This book is the first to present a working framework for dramatherapists, social workers, family and marital therapists, and others conducting groups. This framework primarily deals with dramatherapy in the non-clinical setting such as family centres, residential childrens' homes, social services resources and intermediate treatment centres.

Jennings, Sue (Ed.). *Dramatherapy. Theory and Practice for Teachers and Clinicians.* HB. This book is intended as a definitive text for the clinical practicioner or teacher who wishes to use role-play and enactment in the context of therapeutic work. It is not therefore written just for the dramatherapist but for all whose work involves the subject.

Jennings, Sue, Cattanach, Ann, Mitchell, Steve, Chesner, Anna and Meldrum, Brenda. *The Handbook of Dramatherapy*. Provides a comprehensive base for theory and practice and will be an invaluable resource for all mental health professionals as well as for students of dramatherapy and theatre.

Johansen, Mila. *101 Theatre Games for Drama Teachers, Classroom Teachers and Directors*. A workbook that can be used by randomly selecting a game or in an on-going classroom or workshop situation, starting at the beginning and systematically going through to the end.

Kaplan, Dr. Babette. *Drama and Creativity in Action. Teacher's Handbook*. The intention of this book is to provide a resource for teachers, which is not too threatening but will encourage them to take the risk to try new activities, to be open-minded and have an emphasis on individuality and not sameness or conformity.

Kelner, Lenore Blank. *Creative Classroom. A Guide for Using Creative Drama in the Classroom, Pre K-6*. Provides teachers with a number of creative drama strategies for use in the classroom, on a daily basis and across the curriculum.

Kelsal, Malcolm. *Studying Drama. An Introduction*. Here, genre, character and ideology are examined at length. The extensive use of examples, and the concern with debate, make this book both stimulating to the individual and very practical for use in discussion groups.

Kempe, Andy. *The GCSE Drama Coursebook*. The work here is firmly based on practical explorations of how to make, perform and appreciate plays, and it uses the widest possible range of approaches to drama, including research, improvisation, text study, critical analysis, script writing, design, presentation and self-assessment.

Kempe, Andy (Ed.). *Drama Education and Special Needs*. This book presents the practical experiences of a number of teacher who have used drama in their work with young people (5–19 year-olds) who have a wide range of special individual needs. Through reflecting on their own developing practice, the contributors able to recount what they and their students have learned, and to pass it on in a way which will encourage other teachers to try out ideas of their own.

Kempe, A. and Holroyd, R.. *A South African Scrapbook*. Joseph and his daughter Sissie show us their family scrapbook of letters, documents and photographs, giving us the experiences of three generations in South Africa. Imaginative practical tasks help students explore the themes behind the story.

Kempe, Andy and Holroyd, Rick. *Imaging: Resources for English and Drama. A Teacher's Guide*. A highly original resource for teaching English and drama, designed for use with students in the lower years of secondary school. The teacher's book often shows how to work through resources in a structured and creative way and on how to assess student's responses.

Kempe, Andy and Warner, Lionel. *Starting With Scripts. Dramatic Literature for Key Stages 3 and 4*. The authors have provided strategies for teaching the drama requirements of the curriculum for English. It is particularly appropriate for teachers of English who are not drama specialists. Teacher's notes and photocopiable worksheets mean that units can be selected to fit in with existing lesson plans.

King, Nancy. *Storymaking and Drama. An Approach to Teaching Language and Literature at the Secondary and Post Secondary Levels*. Teachers will find in this book thoughtful, practical, inventive, and creative ways to explore literature and drama in the classroom. The book is designed to support teachers as they seek ways to find their own approaches to teaching and learning. The author has included many stories from around the world to make the book a joy to read and help to stimulate the development of new ideas for classroom educational practice.

Kitson, Neil and Spiby, Ian. *Drama 7–11. Developing Primary Teaching Skills*. A practical guide to teaching drama which provides a clear and coherent framework together with a theoretical underpinning which teachers can use to create their own drama lessons.

Krell-Oishi, Mary. *Perspectives. Relative Scenes for Teens*. Twenty-three scenes in five categories: Dating, Pregnancy, Control, Family, Growing Up.

Line, Antoinette. *Drama Lessons in Action*. Resource material for teachers of junior and secondary age pupils with lessons taught through improvisation. These are not presented as 'model lessons' but provide ideas for adaptation and further development.

Linnel, Rosemary. *Practical Drama Handbook*. Structured Coursework and Resource Material for Drama Classes. Appropriate for either a two-year course (particularly at GCSE level) or a concentrated one-year course at senior level. This resource book, with its developmental lesson plans covering the core elements in the subject should be of value to any teacher of drama.

Linnel, Rosemary. *Theatre Arts Workshop*. Offers all theatre arts students a practical and accessible guide to the main topics covered by post-16 syllabuses. The emphasis throughout the book is on the practical, and there is a liberal use made in it of illustrative and textual examples.

Mackey, Sally (Ed.). *Practical Theatre. A Post 16 Approach*. This comprehensive volume covers the practical aspects of the A-Level theatre studies/performing arts syllabuses and GNVQ performing arts. The book seeks to encourage practical work of quality by providing a rigorous framework of knowledge.

McClintock, Ann B. *Drama for Mentally Handicapped Children*. HB. Planned for a relatively small space, with the minimum of special equipment, the activities in this book have all been developed and tested by the author herself, with the childrens' enthusiastic co-operation.

McCullough, Christopher. *Theatre Praxis. Teaching Drama Through Practice*. A collection of essays which do not attempt to instruct people in ways to teach drama, but rather present a lively discourse on a variety of practices. The contributors contend that to practise is to theorise, and to theorise is to practise—a necessary symbiosis which requires an active engagement by each individual, whether they be student or teacher.

McGregor, Lynn, Tate, Maggie and Robinson, Ken. *Learning Through Drama*. Provides a basis for a more throrough understanding of the learning processes involved in drama and for the clear formulation of aims and strategies in the drama lesson itself.

Maley, Alan and Duff, Alan. *Drama Techniques in Language Learning. A Resource Book of Communication Activities for Language Teachers*. This book offers a large selection of techniques for use at all levels which focus learners' attention on communicative tasks or activities. These involve the whole personality of the learner and provide real reasons for expressing feelings and opinions.

Martin, William and Vallins, Gordon. *Routes. Exploration Drama*. Routes contains pictures, stories, songs, ballads, experiments, documentaries and projects for dramatic activity.

Mayne, Andrew and Shuttleworth, John. *Considering Drama.* This book offers a practical and incisive approach to drama criticism for those following advanced (post 16+) courses. suitable both for English Literature students and those studying drama and theatre arts, the book examines how a wide range of critical approaches is appropriate to drama.

Neelands, Jonothan. *Beginning Drama 11–14.* This book provides a positive and accessible account of what teachers need to know, understand and be able to do in order to ensure that their first experiences of drama teaching are controlled, effective and based on the best practices.

Neelands, Jonothan. *Making Sense of Drama. A Guide to Classroom Practice.* This is a straightforward and accessible account of how to approach drama in the classroom. It is based firmly on the most recent thinking of leading drama theorists, but translates their ideas into terms which teachers can use.

Neelands, Jonothan. *Structuring Drama Work. A Handbook of Available Forms in Theatre and Drama.* A practical handbook for drama teachers and youth theatre workers. It offers a whole range of theatrical 'conventions' to help initiate, focus and develop dramatic activity—whether in a workshop situation or as part of an active exploration of texts.

Newbould, Anne and Stibbs, Andrew. *Exploring Texts Through Reading Aloud and Dramatization.* Offers ideas for work on texts to middle and secondary English classes. It will be a valuable source book for teachers who wish to develop oral and dramatic approaches to the teaching and learning of lterature and language.

Newton, Robert G. *Improvisation: Project and Practice.* This book deals with the results obtained from an improvisation course run in a Theatre Club—what went well and what did not. In addition to comments by members of the group and several excercises, many points are taken up dealing with improvisation in general.

Nobleman, Roberta. *50 Proects for Creative Dramatics.* Fifty exercises for young people that have been well-tried and should fire the imagination for more serious work.

Ogden, Chris. *Escape Into Drama.* With reference to National Curriculum criteria, the author presents games, techniques and four drama structures which have been used with primary children from Years 3–6. They are designed to provide half a term's drama work, but could also be used as starting points for other drama.

Ogden, Chris. *First and Best in Education. Further Escapes Into Drama.* The structures in this book are intended to help teachers to address some of the areas mentioned in the programmes of study for English and are designed to build on the children's previous experiences in drama. All of the structures have been used in the primary school and can be freely adapted to suit individual groups.

O'Neill, Cecily. *Drama Worlds. A Framework for Process Drama.* Examines the complex improvised event called process drama and identifies it as an essential part of today's theatre. Cecily O'Neill considers process drama's sources and its connections with more familiar kinds of improvisation.

Orr, Bob and Helen. *Workshop Drama for Secondary Schools.* This book is devoted to the teacher who, willingly or otherwise, agrees to attempt drama in the classroom. Prompt sheets for class discussion, simple exercises and scripts are provided for the childrens' use. Material has been included which will encompass a wide variety of achievement levels. Each chapter contains one or more 'worked example' and a list of suggestions for similar stages of development.

O'Toole, John and Haseman, Brad. *Dramawise. An Introduction to GCSE Drama.* A core coursebook for GCSE Drama and other introductory drama courses. It provides a structured framework for a coherent, sequential course in all the elements of drama.

Peter, Melanie. *Drama for All. Developing Drama in the Curriculum with Pupils with Special Educational Needs.* This book offers a practical developmental approach to drama-in-education based on current mainstream theory and practice, that is acceptable to all beginners in drama—staff as well as pupils—including those students with severe and moderate learning difficulties as well as those with emotional and behavioural difficulties.

Peterson, Lenka and O'Connor, Dan. *Kids Take the Stage. Helping Young People Discover the Creative Outlet of the Theatre.* Foreword by Paul Newman. If you want to direct kids in the constructive activities of putting on shows in drama clubs, churches, and neighbourhood groups—and release the power of their creative potential as well—you'll find this resource invaluable.

Pinnell, Linda. *Getting Started in Theatre.* An introduction to the world of drama and performance. This activity-driven text begins with an historical overview, covering classical through 20th-century theatre. Taking students step-by-step and providing exercises designed to get students involved, Getting Started in Theatre is a wonderful introduction to theatre.

Poisson, Camille L. *Theatre and the Adolescent Actor. Building a Sucessful School Program.* HB. For teachers new to drama, those just beginning their careers, or English teachers being pressed into service because of school budget cuts, this book offers guidance and encouragement through the pitfalls and problems in the secondary school setting.

Polisini, Judith Kase (Ed.). *Drama as a Meaning Maker.* A collection of discussion responses and summaries of group discussions in relation to the 'brain and meaning', 'meaning and the child', and ' The lucid and the ludic'.

Polsky, Milton E. *Let's Improvise. Becoming Creative, Expressive and Spontaneous Through Drama.* 'A gold mine of a book, filled with exciting ideas and materials or the teacher wanting to use drama creatively. The philosophy is sound and the activities fresh and inventive for all levels from elementary school through senior citizens.'—Tom Behm, President, Children's Theatre Association of America.

Rankin, Irené. *Drama 5–14. A Practical Approach to Classroom Drama.* In this book, Rankin has devised easy-to-follow lesson plans, many of which use themes and topics that are already familiar to pupils. By following the clearly presented guidelines for each lesson, teachers will soon build up their confidence in teaching drama, and through this, develop a growing enjoyment in working with their classes.

Rathburn, Amy K. *Taking Centre Stage. Drama In America. Teacher's Manual.* This book provides a historical journey of drama and shows the profound influence of Broadway and the big and small screens on the American experience.

Readman, Geoff and Lamont, Gordon. *Drama. A Handbook for Primary Teachers.* A unique resource for the non-specialist primary teacher. Combining in one volume suggestions for planning, implementation and assessment, as well as practical examples, it shows how drama can enhance the National Curriculum and deepen personal and social skills.

Remocker, A. Jane and Storch, Elizabeth T. *Action Speaks Louder. A Handbook of Structured Group Techniques.* Intended primarily for occupational therapists, this unique book will also prove useful to anyone involved in interpersonal skills training.

Rice-Oxley, M. Andrew. *First and Best in Education. Multi-Purpose Drama/English Workbook Key Stages 3–4.* Versatile material for specialist drama teachers, specialist English teachers, and hybrid English teachers who like to include drama in their teaching programme. Topics for drama, oral work and writing; group work and media work.

Saldana, Johnny. *Drama of Color. Improvisation with Multi-ethnic Folklore.* A unique resource for using drama to enhance K-6 children's ethnic literacy by provoking personal insights into the multi-ethnic world in which we live.

Scanlan, David. *Reading Drama.* An essential guide for students who want to better understand , appreciate, and enjoy the plays they read. It empowers readers with no previous knowledge of the subject to respond fully and creatively to drama in print.

Scarisbrick, George. *Lucky Dip Drama.* A varied collection of short plays for two, three, four or more characters for use in education. There is also an additional group of play scripts for the users to 'add-to, alter and adapt'.

Scher, Anna and Verrall, Charles. *Another 100+ Ideas for Drama.* Following the wide acclaim of 100+ Ideas for Drama this very successful team have produced a second volume of lively and practical suggestions for drama work. Tried and tested at the Anna Scher Children's Theatre in London, it concentrates particularly on developing improvisational skills.

Schotz, Amiel. *Theatre Games and Beyond. A Creative Approach for Performers.* A new teacher's handbook of over 140 theatre games to stimulate creativity in performers of all ages. The essentials of creative acting skills with games and exercises in twelve units.

Self, David. *The Drama and Theatre Arts Course Books.* The book is organised in five sections, each of which explores a major period of theatre development. It also presents a range of material—extracts, illustrations, photographs and original text—selected to provide both a source of reference and a basis for creative work, in all branches of stagecraft.

Shiach, Don. *From Page to Performance. A Study Book for Drama.* Looks at the transformation of a writtten text into a live and dramatic performance. The author stresses drama as a co-operative and performing art, with playwrights, directors, actors, stage managers, and technicians united to bring the text to life.

Smith, Kate. *Take a Lesson in Drama.* This book involves pupils working with others and challenges them with a demanding range of activities that are exciting, interesting and related to their own experiences. The book reflects the requirements of the National Curriculum whilst providing a real source of imaginative material for use with all levels.

Smith, Stuart. *The Primary Drama Handbook.* This origianl book provides a resource book which emphasizes throughout a form of educational drama which encourages children to think, question, and discuss rather than just act out a story. It will be essential reading for all teachers concerned with drama and children's development.

Somers, John. *Drama in the Curriculum.* In this highly illustrated and practical book, John Somers looks at most facets of drama teaching and shows how drama can be a vibrant part of the new curriculum.

Spalding, Peter. *Drama in Practice. A Handbook for Students.* This book provides students of drama and literature with detailed guidance on studying and performing a play in a workshop environment, using simulation as a basic technique. Each chapter analyses a particular play, and is divided into six modular units.

Stoate, Graham. *Dramastarters.* A collection of over two hundred tried and tested ideas for drama games, excercises and improvisations. It contains a wealth of suggestions for drama teachers and will be an invaluable handbook for the non-specialist.

Stoate, Graham. *Themes from Life. A Sampler of Contemporary Drama, with Suggestions for Discussion, Written Work, Improvisation and Practical Drama.* This is an anthology of excerpts from modern plays designed for use in Englsh and drama lessons as well as in social studies and religious education lessons.

Stubbs, Chris. *Drama Works!.* (Classmate Books). This handbook for educational drama is intended for use with students throughout the secondary age range. Whatever your level of experience at teaching drama, there is a wealth of material here for you.

Taylor, Ken (Ed.). *Drama Strategies. New Ideas from London Drama.* A collection of ideas and lessons for drama teaching developed by teachers in the Islington division of London Drama. Including detailed and practical lesson plans giving advice on organising the drama, possible outcomes and dealing with potential problems. Photocopiable pages for use as props where required.

Taylor, Philip. *Researching Drama and Arts Education. Paradigms and Possibilities.* This book examines the major issues in research design for arts educators today and aims to answer two key questions: How might researchers design their studies? What research methods are appropriate for specific investigative questions?.

Theodorou, Michael. *Ideas that Work in Drama.* A book of practical ideas for work with drama classes and groups aged 11 to 18 The ideas are presented in careful stages in the sort of simple, direct language that teachers themselves will use to stimulate work in the classroom.

Thistle, Louise. *Dramatizing Aesop's Fables. Creative Scripts For The Elementary Classroom.* A clear and simple guide to familiarise teachers and children with classic literature through the narrative-mime approach. Eight adapted and scripted fables, twenty-seven additional suggestions with discussion material.

Thistle, Louise. *Dramatizing Myths and Tales. Creating Plays For Large Groups.* Explore the richness and diversity of five cultures—West African, Mayan, Native American, Japanese and British—as you create your own classroom production with storytellers, a sound crew, actors and props.

Thorn, Gill. *Make Your Own Model Theatre. Putting on a Play.* Illus. by Terry Burton. This book tells you how to make a beautiful stage out of two breakfast cereal boxes. There are also stories, scenery and characters for four different plays that you can out on: Jungle Adventure, Mission in Space, Fishy Business and Haunted House. Each play is colour coded and there are ideas for stage lighting and special effects to impress your audience.

Tomlinson, Richard. *Disability, Theatre and Education.* This book addresses the idea of theatre as a means of communication between disabled and able bodied people. The book will help those interested in setting up groups for disabled actors similar to the authors' own Graeae Theatre Company.

van Ments, Morry. *The Effective Use of Role-play. A Handbook for Teachers and Trainers.* HB. This book, designed for teachers and lecturers, shows how the technique of role-play can best be used in the transmission of knowledge in education and training.

It sets forth a range of role-play methods together with the benefits and disadvantages of each system.

Walker, Lois. *Readers Theatre in the Middle School and Junior High Classroom.* A take part teacher's guide for using Readers Theatre as a springboard to language development. What is Readers Theatre? Readers Theatre strategies; four specialized in-class applications for Readers Theatre; casting, staging, and performing the readings; two sample Readers Theatre scripts.

Way, Brian. *Audience Participation: Theatre for Young People.* This highly experienced playwright, director and teacher writes about: family audiences in conventional theatres with fixed seating; approaches to many different forms of open staging; details of participation for confined age-groups and controlled numbers in the open stage and the approach of director and the actor to children's theatre with audience participation.

Winston, Joe and Tandy, Miles. *Beginning Drama 4–11.* This book provides an introduction for early years and primary school teachers new to drama. It offers step-by-step guidance to help teachers and children grow in confidence in their use of drama and provides a range of strategies to help with planning, guiding and controlling a drama lesson.

Woolland, Brian. *The Teaching of Drama in the Primary School.* A lively and readable book which offers a unique blend of theory and practice. The book assumes no previous knowledge of teaching drama and will therefore be useful to trainee teachers and in-service teachers wanting to make use of drama in their daily teaching.

Further Reading

Stagecraft

Druxman, Michael B. *The Art of Storytelling*. This is an excellent introduction to the art and craft of storytelling. Aimed primarily at the student and the beginner, it focuses on the structure of the screenplay to explore the essentials of a dynamic narrative—set-up, catalyst, turning-point, climax, confrontation and resolution. Drawing heavily on mainstream popular cinema for example and illustration, *The Art of Storytelling* is both appealing and accessible.

Acting and Directing

Bartow, Arthur (1988). *The Director's Voice: Twenty-One Interviews*. Paperback.
Bauer, Caroline Feller. *Presenting Reader's Theater: Plays and Poems to Read Aloud*. Hardcover.
Bernardi, Philip. *Improvisation Starters: A Collection of 900 Improvisation Situations for the Theater*. Paperback.
Billington, Michael. *One Night Stands: Critic's View of British Theatre, 1971–91*. Cloth and paperback.
Blumenthal, Eileen and Taymor, Julie (1995) *Julie Taymor, Play With Fire: Theater Opera Film*. Hardcover.
Bly, Mark et al. (Eds.) (1996). *The Production Notebooks: Theatre in Process (Theatre in Process, Vol 1)*. Paperback.
Boal, Augusto. *Games for Actors and Non-Actors*. Paperback.
Boal, Augusto, Jackson, Adrian (Translator). *The Rainbow of Desire: The Boal Method of Theatre and Therapy*. Paperback.
Bray, Errol. *Playbuilding/a Guide for Group Creation of Plays With Young People*. Paperback.
Brook, Peter (1994). *The Shifting Point: 1946–1987*. Paperback.
Brown, Shirley. *Bristol Old Vic Theatre School*. Paperback.
Burian, Jarka. *The Secret of Theatrical Space – the Memoir of Josef Svoboda*. Paperback.
Callow, Simon and Osborne, Helen. *National Theatre Book*. Cloth and paperback.
Carey, Dean. *Masterclass; v.1: Men*. Paperback.
Carey, Dean. *Masterclass; v.2: Women*. Paperback.
Cassady, Marsh Gary. *Acting Games: Improvisations and Exercises: A Textbook of Theatre Games and Improvisations*. Paperback.
Chayefsky, Terry. *Acting in Prime Time: The Mature Person's Guide to Breaking into Show Business*. Paperback.
Chekhov, Michael and Gordon, Mel. *On the Technique of Acting: The First Complete Edition of Chekhov's Classic to the Actor*. Paperback.
Clurman, Harold (1997). *On Directing*. Paperback.
Cohen, Edward M. *Working on a New Play: A Play Development Handbook for Actors, Directors, Designers and Playwrights*. Paperback.
Cole, Toby (Compiler). *Acting: A Handbook of the Stanislavski Method*. Paperback.
Cole, Toby et al. (Ed.). *Actors on Acting: The Theories, Techniques, and Practices of the World's Great Actors, Told in Their Own Words*. Paperback.

Converse, Terry John (1995). *Directing for the Stage: A Workshop Guide of 42 Creative Training Exercises and Projects*. Paperback.
Craig, David. *On Singing Onstage (Applause Acting Series)*. Paperback.
Michael Coveney *The Citz*. Paperback.
Dean, Alexander and Carra, Lawrence (1988). *Fundamentals of Play Directing*. Hardcover.
Donnellan, Declan. *Acting the Truth*. Paperback.
Dixon, Michael Bigelow and Smith, Joel A. (1995). *Anne Bogart: Viewpoints (Career Development Series)*. Paperback.
Douthitt, Chris and Wiecks, Tom. *Voice Overs: Putting Your Mouth Where the Money Is*. Paperback.
Duff, Charles. *Lost Summer: Heyday of the West End Theatre*. Paperback.
Eyre, Richard etc. *Guys and Dolls Book*. Paperback.
Grandstaff, Russell J. (1989). *Acting and Directing*. Paperback.
Green, Michael. *The Art of Course Acting*. A wonderfully funny and silly guide of particular value to those thespians whose enthusiasm exceeds their talent. *The Art of Course Acting* has been required reading in both professional and amateur theatre for almost thirty years, and is presented here in a revised and updated edition. Paperback.
Gurchakov, Nikolai and Gorchakov, Kikolai, (1985). *Stanislavsky Directs*. Paperback.
Henry, Mari Lyn and Rogers, Lynne. *How to Be a Working Actor: The Insider's Guide to Finding Jobs in Theater, Film, and Television*. Paperback.
Herman, Lewis and Herman Marguerite Shalett. *American Dialects: A Manual for Actors, Directors, and Writers*. Paperback.
Hunt, Albert and Reeves, Geoffrey (1995). *Peter Brook (Directors in Perspective)*. Paperback.
Jacobson, Deborah. *Survival Jobs: 118 Ways to Make Money While Pursuing Your Dreams*. Paperback.
Jones, David Richard (1987). *Great Directors at Work: Stanislavsky, Brecht, Kazan, Brook*. Paperback.
Joseph, Erik. *Glam Scam: Successfully Avoiding the Casting Couch and Other Talent and Modeling Scams*. Paperback.
Karshner, Roy, Karshner, Roger and Stern, David Alan. *Dialect Monologues*.
Kissel, Howard (1993). *David Merrick: The Abominable Snowman: The Unauthorized Biography*. Hardcover.
Leiter, Samuel L. (1994). *The Great Stage Directors: 100 Distinguished Careers of the Theater*. Hardcover.
Lewenstein, Oscar (1995). *Kicking Against the Pricks: A Theatre Producer Looks Back: The Memoirs of Oscar Lewenstein*. Hardcover.
McGrath, John. *Good Night Out*. Paperback.
Marker, Lise-Lone and Marker, Frederick J. (1992). *Ingmar Bergman: A Life in the Theatre (Directors in Perspective)*. Paperback.
Marowitz, Charles (1991). *Directing the Action: Acting and Directing in the Contemporary Theatre (The Applause Acting Series)*. Paperback.
Miller, Scott. *From Assassins to West Side Story: The Director's Guide to Musical Theatre*. The book discusses 16 musicals – Assassins, Cabaret, Carousel, Company, Godspell, Gypsy, How to Succeed, Into the Woods, Jesus Christ Superstar, Les Miserables,

Man of La Mancha, Merrily We Roll Along, My Fair Lady, Pippin, Sweeney Todd, and West Side Story. Each chapter takes one musical and dissects it – focusing on textual and musical themes, ways in which the production design can support those themes, insight into the motivations and backstories of characters, the historical and social context of the action, the creators' intentions, the subtext of the book and lyrics, the show's relevance to our contemporary world, and other pertinent information. Paperback.

Nicholas, Michael Saint. *An Actor's Guide: Your First Year in Hollywood*. Paperback.

Novak, Deborah and Novak, Elaine Adams (1996). *Staging Musical Theatre*. Paperback.

Alison Oddey (1997) *Devising Theatre: A Practical and Theoretical Handbook*. Paperback.

Oppenheim, Lois (Ed.) (1997). *Directing Beckett (Theater – Theory-Text-Performance Series)*. Hardcover.

Redgrave, Michael. *Actor's Ways and Means*. Paperback.

Reilly, Andrew. *An Actor's Business: How Show Business Works & How to Market Yourself As an Actor (No Matter Where You Live)*. Paperback.

Richards, Thomas and Grotowski, Jerzy (1995). *At Work With Grotowski on Physical Actions*. Paperback.

Roland, David. *Confident Performer*. Paperback.

Romain, Michael (1992). *A Profile of Jonathan Miller*. Paperback.

Saks, Sol. *Funny Business: the Craft of Comedy Writing*. Paperback.

Seyler, Athene and Scales, Prunella. *Craft of Comedy*. An exchange of Letters on comedy acting techniques. Paperback.

Sher, Antony. *Characters*. Cloth and paperback.

Stafford-Clark, Max. *Letters to George: The Account of a Rehearsal*. Paperback.

Stanislavski, Constantine *et al. An Actor Prepares*. Paperback.

Stanislavski, Constantine *et al. Building a Character*. Paperback.

Tushingham, David (Ed.). *My Perfect Theatre*. Paperback.

Tushingham, David (Ed.). *All Our Own Work*. Paperback.

Tynan, Kenneth and Tynan, Kathleen (Ed.). *Profiles*. Paperback.

Walne, Graham. *Projection for the Performing Arts (Live Performance Technology Series)*. Paperback.

Walne, Graham and Aveline, Lee. *Effects for the Theatre*. Paperback.

Whelan, Jeremy. *New School Acting: Taking It to the Next Level*. Paperback.

Zaporah, Ruth. *Action Theater: The Improvisation of Presence*. Paperback.

Zadan, Craig. *Sondheim & Co*. Paperback.

Stage Lighting and Design

Aronson, Arnold. *American Set Design*. Paperback.

Jarka Burian *The Secret of Theatrical Space – the Memoir of Josef Svoboda*. Paperback.

Barrell, Kay M. *The Technical Production Handbook: A Guide for Performing Arts Presenting Organizations and Touring Companies*. Paperback.

Cohen, Edward M. *Working on a New Play: A Play Development Handbook for Actors, Directors, Designers & Playwrights*. Paperback.

Cunningham, Glen. *Stage Lighting Revealed: A Design and Execution Handbook*. Hardcover.

Fraser, Neil. *Lighting and Sound (A Phaidon Theater Manual)*. Paperback.

Hays, David. *Light on the Subject: Stage Lighting for Directors and Actors and the Rest of Us*. Paperback.
Miller, James Hull. *Stage Lighting in the Boondocks: A Layman's Handbook of Down-To-Earth Methods of Lighting Theatricals With Limited Resources*. Paperback.
Nelms, Henning. *Scene Design: A Guide to the Stage*. Paperback.
Pecktal, Lynn. *Designing and Drawing for the Theatre*. Hardcover.
Pilbrow, Richard. *Stage Lighting*. Cloth.
Reid, Francis. *Lighting the Stage: A Lighting Designer's Experiences*. Paperback.
Reid, Francis. *The Stage Lighting Handbook*. Paperback.
Smith, Ronn. *American Set Design Two*. Paperback.
Sweet, Harvey. *Handbook of Scenery, Properties, and Lighting: Lighting Vol 2*. Paperback.

Costume

Bentley, Toni. *Costumes by Karinska*. Hardcover.
Dearing, Shirley. *Elegantly Frugal Costumes!: The Poor Man's Do-It-Yourself Costume Maker's*. Paperback.
Ingham, Rosemary and Covey, Elizabeth. *The Costume Designer's Handbook: A Complete Guide for Amateur and Professional Costume Designers*. Paperback.
Kidd, Mary T. *Stage Costume Step-By-Step: The Complete Guide to Designing and Making Stage Costumes for All Major Drama Periods and Genres*. Hardcover.
Litherland, Janet et al. Broadway Costumes on a Budget: Big-time Ideas for Amateur Producers. Paperback.
Payne, Blanche et al. *History of Costume: From the Ancient Mesopotamians to the Twentieth Century*. Hardcover.

Make-up

Baygan, Lee. *Makeup for Theatre, Film & Television: A Step-By-Step Photographic Guide*. Paperback.
Corson, Richard. *Stage Makeup*. Hardcover.
Delamar, Penny. *The Complete Make-Up Artist: Working in Film, Television and Theatre*. Paperback.
Kohoe, Vincent J. R. *The Technique of the Professional Make-Up Artist*. Paperback.
Swinfield, Rosemarie. *Stage Makeup Step-By-Step: The Complete Guide to Basic Makeup, Planning and Designing Makeup, Adding and Reducing Age, Ethnic Makeup, Special effects*. Paperback.

Props

Rump, Nan. *Puppets and Masks: Stagecraft and Storytelling*. Paperback.
Sweet, Harvey. *Handbook of Scenery, Properties, and Lighting: Lighting Vol 2*. Paperback.
Thurston, James. *The Prop Builder's Mask-Making Handbook*. Paperback.
Thurston, James. *The Prop Builder's Molding and Casting Handbook*. Paperback.
Thurston, James. *The Theater Props Handbook: A Comprehensive Guide to Theater Properties, Materials, and Construction*. Paperback.

Stage Management

Aronson, Arnold. *American Set Design*. Paperback.

Barrell, Kay M. *The Technical Production Handbook: A Guide for Performing Arts Presenting Organizations and Touring Companies*. Paperback.

Miller, James Hull. *Small Stage Sets on Tour: A Practical Guide to Portable Stage Sets*. Paperback.

Ionazzi, Daniel A. *The Stagecraft Handbook*. The Stagecraft Handbook strives to be lightweight, compact, and economical. Daniel Ionazzi leaves the specifics to the designers, but provides practical, reliable advice for those involved in setting the stage. With chapters on tools, scale drawings, scenic materials, joinery, flats, and rigging to fly, Ionazzi provides valuable know-how to help novice and experienced stagecrafters create their dream sets within practical boundaries of time and money. Paperback.

Lord, William H. *Stagecraft 1: A Complete Guide to Backstage Work*. Paperback.

Menear, Pauline. *Stage Management and Theatre Administration (Phaidon Theater Manuals)*. Paperback.

Nelms, Henning. *Scene Design: A Guide to the Stage*. Paperback.

Smith, Ronn. *American Set Design Twp*. Paperback.

Stage Fighting

Girard, Dale Anthony. *Actors on Guard: A Practical Guide for the Use of the Rapier and Dagger for Stage and Screen*. Paperback.

Hobbs, William. *Fight Direction for Stage and Screen*. Paperback.

Suddeth, Allen J. *Fight Directing for the Theatre*. Paperback.

Play and Screenwriting

Aitchity, Kenneth and Wong, Chi-Li. *Writing Treatments That Sell*. Much praised Guide on how to create and market your story ideas to the Motion Picture and Television industry. Paperback.

Brook, Peter. *The Empty Space*. Paperback.

Cooper, Dona. *Writing Great Screenplays*. Paperback.

Druxman, Michael B. *How to Write Any Story: The Art of Storytelling*. This is an excellent introduction to the art and craft of storytelling. Aimed primarily at the student and the beginner, it focuses on the structure of the screenplay to explore the essentials of a dynamic narrative – set-up, catalyst, turning-point, climax, confrontation and resolution. Drawing heavily on mainstream popular cinema for example and illustration, *The Art of Storytelling* is both appealing and accessible.

Field, Syd. *Screenplay: The Foundations of Screenwriting*. Paperback.

Field, Syd. *Selling a Screenplay*. Paperback.

Hauge, Michael. *How to Write and Sell Your Screenplay*.

Hauge, Michael. *Writing Screenplays That Sell*. Paperback.

Horton, Andrew. *Writing the Character-centered Screenplay*. Cloth.

Sautter, Carl. *How to Sell Your Screenplay: The Real Rules of Film and Television*. Paperback.

Singer, Dana. *The Stagewriter's Handbook*. A much recommended business guide for Playwrights, Composers, Lyricists and Librettists.

Sova, Kathy *et al.* (Eds) (1996). *Dramatists Sourcebook: 1996–97*. Paperback.
Sweet, Jeff. *The Dramatist's Toolkit: The Craft of the Working Playwright*.
Turner, B. (Ed.). *The Writer's Handbook – UK Edition*. Published annually by Writer's Digest, listing contact details of thousands of potential markets. Paperback.
Various *The Writers' & Artists' Yearbook 1998: A Directory for Writers, Artists, Playwrights, Writers for Film, Radio (91st Ed)*. Paperback.

In the past it seemed that there were very few plays for young people, but nowadays you can find quite a number.

The following plays are grouped by theme; the descriptions, age ranges and so on are their own. The list is far from exhaustive, and further information can be obtained from:

Dramatic Exchange
//www.dramaex.org.uk

Internet Bookshop
//www.stageplays.com

Music Line
18 Cadogan Road
Dosthill
Tamworth B77 1PQ
Tel: 01827 281431
Fax: 01827 284214
musiclinepublications@btinternet.com

Samuel French
52 Futzroy Street
London W1P 6JR
Tel: 0171 387 0373
Fax: 0171 387 2161
//www.samuelfrench-london.co.uk

Warner Chappell
129 Park Street
London W1Y 3FA

Play List

Mock Horror/Gothic

Title	Author	Source	Length	Age range	Characters	Description
The Rocky Horror Show		Music Line	2 hours	11-18 years		Musical
The Rocky Horror Show		Music Line	1 hour	7–12 years		Musical
Dracula	Charles McKeown	Warner Chappell		Teenage		Thriller
Dracula	Jane Thornton/ John Gobber	Warner Chappell		Young Adult		Thriller
The Curse of the Egyptian Mummy		Internet Bookshop			11 Characters	Adventure
I Was A Teenage Jekyll & Hyde	Randall Newton	Internet Bookshop			11 Principals	Play with Music
The Monster That Ate 3B	Randall Newton	Internet Bookshop			25 Characters	Adventure
Percival Plum in Monsterland	Mike Lambe/ Ray Gay	Internet Bookshop			16 Roles	Adventure/ Romance
The Thwarting of Baron Bolligrew	Robert Bolt	Internet Bookshop/ Samuel French				Drama
Wyrd Sisters	Stephen Briggs	Internet Bookshop			Large Cast	Comedy (Adapted from Terry Pratchett)
The Curse of the Labyrinth	Brian Hayles	Samuel French			7 Characters	Horror

Miscellaneous

Title	Author	Source	Length	Age range	Characters	Description
The Seven Sided Dice		Music Line	2 hours	11–18 years		Musical
King of Sunset Town	Christopher Blankley	Dramatic Exchange		Young Teenage		Tragi-Comedy
Daydreams or Jack London & The Oyster Pirates	Tom Blow	Dramatic Exchange		Young Teenage		Musical
A Wildwood Reunion	Jonathon Kalindas	Dramatic Exchange		Teenage/ Young Adult		Drama
The Children's Home	William Hellman	Warner Chappell		Teenage		Drama
The Day of the Demon Bowler	Georgina Reid	Warner Chappell				Comedy
Escapade	Roger McDougall	Warner Chappell				Comedy
Alan and the King's Daughters	Helen Murdoch	Samuel French				Musical

Title	Author	Source	Length	Age range	Characters	Description
The Burnston Drum	Ellen Dryden/ Don Taylor/ Charles Young	Internet Bookshop			24 Principals	Musical
Daisy Pulls It Off	Denise Deegan	Internet Bookshop			16 Principals	Drama
Donald and the Dragon	Dorothy Carr	Internet Bookshop			18 Principals	Fantasy
Dreamjobs	Graham Jones	Internet Bookshop			5 Principals	Drama
Dreams of Ann Frank	Bernard Kops	Internet Bookshop/ Samuel French			8 Principals	Drama
Hans, The Witch & The Goblin	Alan Cullen	Internet Bookshop			13 Principals	Fantasy
The Roses of Eyam	Don Taylor	Internet Bookshop			Large Cast	Drama
Stove Soup	Paul Thain	Internet Bookshop/ Samuel French			Large Cast	Drama
Orsin in Tir nan Org	Eve Ferguson	Dramatic Exchange				Drama
Mr Macaroni & The Exploding Pizza Pie	John Gardiner/ Fitz Coleman	Samuel French			16 Characters	Drama
Dinosaura & All That Rubbish	David Wood & Peter Pontzen	Samuel French			Large Cast	Musical Play (Adapted from Michael Foreman)
The Incredible Vanishing	Denise Coffey	Samuel French			9 Characters	Fantasy

Lewis Carroll

Title	Author	Source	Length	Age range	Characters	Description
Alice's Adventures Through the Looking Glass	Clemence Dane	Internet Bookshop/ Samuel French				Musical Play
Alice Through the Looking Glass		Music Line	2 hours	11–18 years		Musical
Alice in Wonderland		Music Line	1 hour 10 mins	8–12 years		Musical
Alice Through the Looking Glass		Music Line	1 hour	7–11 years		Musical

Charles Dickens

Title	Author	Source	Length	Age range	Characters	Description
Ebenezer		Music Line	1 hour	7–11 years		Musical
David Copperfield	Ian Mullins	Warner Chappell		Teenage/ Young Adult		Drama

Great Expectations	Barbara Field	Warner Chappell				Light Drama
The Life & Adventures of Nicholas Nickleby	David Edgar	Warner Chappell				Light Drama
Copperfield & Co	Frank Kirwin	Warner Chappell (Musicals)				Musical Drama
A Christmas Carol	John Mortimer	Internet Bookshop				Drama
A Christmas Carol	Christopher Bedloe	Samuel French			Large Cast	Musical Play
A Christmas Carol	Shaun Sutton	Samuel French			Large Cast	Chrismas Play

Classically Based

Title	Author	Source	Length	Age range	Characters	Description
Megabyte Warrior (Mozart's Magic Flute)		Music Line	2 hours	11–18 years		Musical

Younger Classics

Title	Author	Source	Length	Age range	Characters	Description
The Pied Piper		Music Line	2 hours	11–18 years		Musical
A Handful of Stars (The Little Match Girl)	Based on Hans Christian Anderson story	Music Line	2 hours	11–18 years		Musical
The Pied Piper		Music Line	1 hour	7–11 years		Musical
The Wind in the Willows		Music Line	1 hour	7–12 years		Musical
Beauty and the Beast	Nicholas Stuart Gray	Warner Chappell				Fantasy
Garvain and the Green Knight		Warner Chappell				Fantasy
The Hunter and the Hen Wife		Warner Chappell				Fantasy
The Imperial Knightingale		Warner Chappell				Fantasy
The Marvellous Tale of Puss in Boots		Warner Chappell				Fantasy
New Clothes for the Emporer		Warner Chappell				Fantasy
New Lamps for Old		Warner Chappell				Fantasy
The Other Cinderella		Warner Chappell				Fantasy
The Princess & The Swineherd		Warner Chappell				Fantasy

The Seventh Swan		Warner Chappell				Fantasy
The Stone Cage		Warner Chappell				Fantasy
The Tinder Box		Warner Chappell				Fantasy
The Adventures of a Bear Called Paddington	Alfred Bradley	Samuel French		Upper Primary		
Aesop's Fables	Peter Terson	Samuel French		Upper Primary		Fantasy
The Gingerbread Man	David Wood	Internet Bookshop			6 Principals	Magical Play
Mr A's Amazing Maze Plays	Alan Aykbourn	Internet Bookshop			8 Roles	Magical Play
My Very Own Story	Alan Aykbourn	Internet Bookshop			13 Roles	Drama
The Nightingale & The Emporer	Alfred Bradley	Internet Bookshop			8 Roles	Fantasy
Old Father Time	David Wood	Internet Bookshop			30 Roles	Play With Music
Our Day Out	Willy Russell/ Bob Eaton/ Chris Mellor	Internet Bookshop/ Samuel French			29 Roles	Play With Music
Peter Pan	J M Barrie/ Piers Charter-Robinson	Internet Bookshop			25 Roles	Drama/Play/ Musical
Toad of Toad Hall	A A Milne/H Fraser Simpson	Internet Bookshop				Musical
The Book & The Pussycat Went to See . . .	David Wood/ Sheila Ruskin	Samuel French			14 Characters	Musical Play
The Pied Piper	Adrian Mitchell/Alan Cohen/ Dominic Muldowney	Samuel French			12 Characters	Play with a twist
The Pied Piper	David Woo/ Dave Arthur/ Toni Arthur	Samuel French			28 Characters	Musical Play
Pinocchio	Brian Way	Samuel French			13 Characters	Drama
Puss in Boots	Brian Way	Samuel French			11 Characters	Drama

Morality/Religious/Christian/Christmas

Title	Author	Source	Length	Age range	Characters	Description
Johnny's Smith's Christmas		Music Line	40 mins	7–12 years		Musical

The Last Little Angels		Music Line	40 mins	5–9 years		Musical
Back to Angels		Music Line	50 mins	7–11 years		Musical
The Good, The Bad and The Donkey		Music Line	45 mins	7–11 years		Musical
The Little Shepherd		Music Line	45 mins	6–11 years		Musical
Pictures of a Christmas World		Music Line	50 mins	6–11 years		Musical
Pictures of Christmas		Music Line	1 hour	6–12 years		Musical
Follow the Star	Jim Parker/ Wally K Daly	Warner Chappell (Musicals)				Musical
Make Me A World	Jim Parker/ Wally K Daly	Warner Chappell (Musicals)				Musical
Moments of Christmas	Trisha Ward	Warner Chappell (Musicals)				Musical
The Children's Crusade	Paul Thompson	Internet Bookshop				Drama
Everyman	Constance Cox	Internet Bookshop			11 Principals	Drama
Lords of Creation	John Wiles	Internet Bookshop			75 roles	Drama
The Divine Short Family	Eric Ferguson	Dramatic Exchange				Comic Nativity

Morality/Religious/Christmas

Title	Author	Source	Length	Age range	Characters	Description
Christmas Crackers	Willis Hall	Samuel French			9 Characters	Children's Play
Good King Wenceslas & The Chancellor of Bohemia	Tony Horitz	Samuel French			15 Characters	Drama
Kidnapped at Christmas	Willis Hall	Samuel French			9 Characters	Drama
The Nativity	Adapted by Angela Black	Samuel French			22 Characters	Miracle Play
A Right Christmas Caper	Willis Hall	Samuel French			9 Characters	Drama

Difficult Issues

Title	Author	Source	Length	Age range	Characters	Description
High	Jonathon Calindas	Dramatic Exchange		Young Adult		Drama (Suicide)
Generation Sex	Lawrence Carr	Dramatic Exchange		Teenage		Drama (Aids/ HIV)

Positive	Lawrence Carr	Dramatic Exchange		Teenage		Drama (HIV)
Little Victories	Shaun Prendergast	Internet Bookshop				Drama (Cancer/ Death)
Zigger Zagger	Peter Terson	Samuel French			Large Cast	Urban Society (Social Issues)

Science Fiction

Title	Author	Source	Length	Age range	Characters	Description
Other Planets	Greg Younger	Dramatic Exchange		Teenage/ Young Adults		Drama
An Alien Stole My Skateboard	Randall Newton	Internet Bookshop				Musical

Shakespearean Based

Title	Author	Source	Length	Age range	Characters	Description
Juliet & Romeo (Romeo & Juliet)	Wayne Anthony	Dramatic Exchange		Teenage/ Young Adult		Drama
The Clown's Macbeth (Macbeth)	Wayne Anthony	Dramatic Exchange		Teenage/ Young Adult		Comedy
The Complete Works of William Shakespeare (Abrgd)	Adam Long/ Daniel Singer/ Jess Winfield	Warner Chappell	97 mins	Teenage		Comedy
The Droitwitch Discovery	Nick Warburton	Internet Bookshop			6 Principals	Drama/ Comedy
The 15 Minute Hamlet	Tom Stoppard	Internet Bookshop			6 Principals	Drama/ Comedy

Classic Theatre

Title	Author	Source	Length	Age range	Characters	Description
An Enemy of the People	Ibsen (Adapted—Arthur Miller)	Warner Chappell			13 Principals	Drama
The Beggar's Opera	John Gray/ David Turner	Warner Chappell (Musical)			5 Principals	Musical/ Drama
Antigone & Other Plays	John Andovilm	Internet Bookshop				Drama
The Bald Prima Donna	Ionesco	Internet Bookshop				Absurd Drama
Caucasian Chalk Circle	Bertolt Brecht	Internet Bookshop				Drama
The Crucible	Arthur Miller	Internet Bookshop				Drama

Stage Adaptations of Known Literary Works

Title	Author	Source	Length	Age range	Characters	Description
The Grapes of Wrath	Frank Galati	Warner Chappell				Drama
Of Mice and Men	John Steinbeck	Warner Chappell				Drama
The Pilgrim's Progress	Trisha Ward	Warner Chappell (Musicals)				Musical Drama
The Three Musketeers	Friml/Grey/ Wodehouse	Warner Chappell (Musicals)				Drama
Twelve Musical Plays for Children	Henry Tobias/ David Ormont	Warner Chappell (Musicals)				Moral (Adapted from famous fairy tales)
Animal Farm	Peter Hall/ Adrian Mitchell/ Richard Peaslea	Internet Bookshop				Drama
Beowulf	Kenneth Picking/Keith Cole	Internet Bookshop				Musical Drama
The Dumb Waiter	Harold Pinter	Internet Bookshop			2 Principals	Drama
The Jungle Book	John Hartoch	Internet Bookshop			13+ Principals	Drama
The Lion, The Witch & The Wardrobe	Glyn Robbins	Internet Bookshop			8 Principals	Drama
A Little Princess	Michael Wild	Internet Bookshop			26 Characters	Drama
Treasure Island	Willis Hall/ Denis King	Internet Bookshop			Large Cast	Musical
The Wind in the Willows	Willis Hall	Internet Bookshop			15+ Roles	Musical
Winnie the Pooh	Glyn Robbins	Internet Bookshop			11 Roles	Drama
The Wizard of Oz	Alfred Bradley	Internet Bookshop			13+ Roles	Musical
The Nightingale & The Emporer's New Clothes	David Hollywood	Dramatic Exchange				Musical

Stage Adaptation

Title	Author	Source	Length	Age range	Characters	Description
The Railway Children	Dave Simpson	Samuel French			10 Characters	Drama (Adapted from E Nesbit)
Telling Wilde Tales	Jules Tasca	Samuel French			Large Cast	Drama (Adapted from Oscar Wilde)

Three Musketeers	Brian Way	Samuel French			14 Characters	Drama
Treasure Island	Willis/Denis King	Samuel French			19 Characters	Drama (Adapted from R L Stevenson)
The Jungle Book	John Hartock	Samuel French			Min. 13 Characters	Drama
The Wizard of Oz	Alfred Bradley	Samuel French			13 Characters	Drama (Adapted from L Frank Baun)
Worzel Gummidge	Keith Waterhouse/ Willis Hall/ Denis King	Samuel French			18 Characters	Musical Play (Adapted from Euphan Todd)

Environmental

Title	Author	Source	Length	Age range	Characters	Description
Whale	David Holman	Samuel French			Large Cast	Drama

Standard Musicals

Title	Author	Source	Length	Age range	Characters	Description
Caroline	Peter Pinne/ Battye	Warner Chappell (Musicals)		Teenage		Drama
Family Rondo	Vera Heade/ Dennis Athison	Warner Chappell (Musicals)				Drama
Smuggle Me A Secret	Vera Heade/ Dennis Athison	Warner Chappell (Musicals)				Drama

Pantomime

Title	Author	Source	Length	Age range	Characters	Description
Aladdin	Betty Astell	Samuel French			12 Principals + Chorus	Musical
Cinderella	Betty Astell	Samuel French			16 Principals + Chorus	Musical
Dick Whittington	Betty Astell	Samuel French			13 Principals + Chorus	Musical
Mother Goose	Betty Astell	Samuel French			17 Principals + Chorus	Musical
Queen of Hearts	Betty Astell	Samuel French			12 Principals + Chorus	Musical
The Sleeping Beauty	Betty Astell	Samuel French			15 Principals + Chorus	Musical
Aladdin & His Wonderful Lamp	Alan Brown	Samuel French			21 Characters	Musical
The Babes in the Wood	Alan Brown	Samuel French			25 Characters	Musical

Cinderella	Alan Brown	Samuel French	17+ Principals	Musical
Dick Whittington	Alan Brown	Samuel French	22 Characters	Musical
Puss in Boots	Alan Brown	Samuel French	17 Characters	Musical
Sleeping Beauty	Alan Brown	Samuel French	23 Characters	Musical
Aladdin	P H Adams & Conrad Carter	Samuel French	13 Principals + Chorus	Musical
Alibaba & The Forty Thieves	Trudy West	Samuel French	16 Principals + Chorus	Musical
The Babes in the Wood	S A Polley & Conrad Carter	Samuel French	17 Principals + Chorus	Musical
Beauty & The Beast	Trudy West	Samuel French	9 Principals + Chorus	Musical
Cinderella	P H Adams & Conrad Carter	Samuel French	8 Principals + Chorus	Musical
Dick Whittington	Trudy West	Samuel French	16 Principals + Chorus	Musical
Humpty Dumpty	Trudy West	Samuel French	19 Principals + Chorus	Musical
Jack & The Beanstalk	P H Adams & Conrad Carter	Samuel French	9 Principals + Chorus	Musical
Mother Goose	Trudy West	Samuel French	18 Principals + Chorus	Musical
Puss in Boots	Conrad Carter & Trudy West	Samuel French	16 Principals + Chorus	Musical
Sinbad the Sailor	Pauline Stuart	Samuel French	17 Principals + Chorus	Musical
The Sleeping Beauty	Trudy West	Samuel French	23 Principals + Chorus	Musical
Aladdin	David Cregan	Samuel French	15 Characters	Musical
Beauty & The Beast	David Cregan	Samuel French	12 Characters	Musical
Jack & The Beanstalk	David Cregan	Samuel French	19 Characters	Musical
Red Riding Hood	David Cregan	Samuel French	12 Characters	Musical
Sleeping Beauty	David Cregan	Samuel French	12 Principals	Musical
Aladdin	Crocker & Gilder	Samuel French	14 Principals	Musical
Babes in the Wood	Crocker & Gilder	Samuel French	13 Principals	Musical
Cinderella	Crocker & Gilder	Samuel French	15 Principals	Musical
Dick Whittington	Crocker & Gilder	Samuel French	12 Principals	Musical
Humpty Dumpty	Crocker & Gilder	Samuel French	15 Principals	Musical
Jack & The Beanstalk	Crocker & Gilder	Samuel French	14 Principals	Musical
Mother Goose	Crocker & Gilder	Samuel French	16 Principals	Musical

Puss in Boots	Crocker & Gilder	Samuel French		16 Principals	Musical
Queen of Hearts	Crocker & Gilder	Samuel French		14 Principals	Musical
Red Riding Hood	Crocker & Gilder	Samuel French		13 Principals	Musical
Robinson Crusoe	Crocker & Gilder	Samuel French		12 Principals	Musical
Sinbad the Sailor	Crocker & Gilder	Samuel French		15 Principals	Musical
The Sleeping Beauty	Crocker & Gilder	Samuel French		12 Principals	Musical
Snow White		Music Line	7–11 years		Musical
Dick Whittington	Keith Dawson	Music Line		27 Principals	Musical
Cinderella	Keith Dawson	Music Line		16 Principals	Musical
Sleeping Beauty	Keith Dawson	Music Line		21 Principals	Musical
Aladdin	Keith Dawson	Music Line		19 Principals	Musical
Snow White and the Seven Dwarfs	Keith Dawson	Music Line		15 Principals	Musical
Babes in the Wood	Keith Dawson	Music Line		15 Principals	Musical
Babes in the Wood	Malcolm Sircom	Music Line		16 Principals	Musical
Jack and the Beanstalk	Malcolm Sircom	Music Line		12 Principals	Musical
Mother Goose	Malcolm Sircom	Music Line		15 Principals	Musical
Snow White	Malcolm Sircom	Music Line		17 Principals	Musical
Aladdin	Colin Wakefield/ Kate Edgar	Warner Chappell		10 Principals	Musical
Cinderella	Colin Wakefield/ Kate Edgar	Warner Chappell		10 Principals	Musical
Mother Goose	Colin Wakefield/ Kate Edgar	Warner Chappell		8 Principals	Musical
The Sleeping Beauty	Colin Wakefield/ Kate Edgar	Warner Chappell		10 Principals	Musical
Babes in the Wood	Peter Webster	Warner Chappell		14 Principals	Musical
Dick Turpin	Peter Webster	Warner Chappell		12 Principals	Musical
Peter Panto	Peter Webster	Warner Chappell		9 Principals	Musical